Stolen Lives

Proceeds from this book, after coverage of publication costs, will go to the Aislinn Education & Support Centre for Survivors of Institutional Abuse.

Cover: Clasped hands at Solidarity March with survivors of institutional abuse (Press Association)

Copyright © Bette Browne, 2014

First Published in 2014 by The Manuscript Publisher

ISBN: 978-0-9576729-3-2

A CIP Catalogue record for this book is available from the National Library

Typesetting, page layout and cover design by DocumentsandManuscripts.com

Printed and bound in Ireland

For Anna

FOREWORD

This book has grown from the aftermath of the first national March of Solidarity with survivors of institutional abuse on June 10, 2009, which the late Christine Buckley and I organised with the support of Barnardos, One in Four and the Children's Rights Alliance, after publication of the report by the Commission to Inquire into Child Abuse.

A day after the solidarity march, a Dáil debate opened on the Ryan Report.

The abuse detailed in the report was described by Fine Gael leader Enda Kenny, now An Taoiseach, as *"torture, pure and simple."* Labour leader Eamon Gilmore, now An Tánaiste, said it was *"a stain on the conscience of our nation."* Michael D Higgins, now An tUachtárain, said: *"There is evidence of an institutional collusion that was deep, continuous and sinister in terms of its relationship between church and State."*

The title of the book underlines that through such "collusion" not only were childhoods stolen but the horrors these children suffered blighted their entire lives.

Indeed, it is little wonder that some, like Angela Collins, found their suffering unendurable and died by suicide.

The book captures the voices of 10 survivors, five men and five women, ranging in age from 54 to 87, who describe the unimaginable cruelty they suffered within these State-funded, religious-run institutions, where they were abandoned by the courts of their country and in many cases by their families. They delineate, too, the desolation and despair that haunted their lives forever after leaving these institutions.

Yet thousands of stories will never be told because so many are now dead. No book can ever tell the whole story, nor does this book attempt to do so. Rather, it is a representative record, told by the survivors themselves, of one of the darkest chapters in Ireland's history.

The names of those who inflicted abuse on the survivors were given to me. Since it has not been possible, however, to ascertain if all of these people are dead or to put the issues to those who may be still alive I have not identified them in any way due to legal constraints.

The Christian Brothers, through Province Leader Br. Kevin Mullan, were "not in a position to furnish information" as to whether certain Brothers were still alive to respond to allegations nor did he proffer a reason or reasons for not providing such information.

In this regard, it would appear that some attitudes have little changed in the intervening five years since the Ryan Report. Indeed, it brought to mind remarks by then Deputy Alan Shatter, former Minister for Justice and Defence, during the Dáil debate on the report in 2009, when he said the following:

> *"In dealing with allegations before the redress board, various religious orders, in particular the Christian Brothers, were in denial up to five days before the report was published. The Christian Brothers' response was that the congregation did not accept that systemic abuse took place. This was the order's standard response, until the Ryan commission report was published…"*

I hope this book will help to ensure that we will never forget the courage of these survivors against such odds and the crimes that this State allowed to be perpetrated against them.

Those who have told their stories in *Stolen Lives* are owed a huge debt of gratitude for their courage in reliving the horrors they suffered and the nightmares they still endure.

I would like to acknowledge especially their foremost champion, the late Christine Buckley, for her unstinting support with this book, which she hoped would be completed for this 5th anniversary of the Ryan Commission report.

Ar deis Dé go raibh a anam dílis.

Bette Browne
May 20, 2014

CONTENTS

1
STORY OF MARY COLLINS
"The fear goes in through the back of my head"

Tower Bridge stands majestically in the morning sunlight above the Saturday strollers along the Thames embankment. Among them an attractive woman stands out, her face framed by flowing black hair. Mary Collins is admiring the morning scene in the city of London that she now calls home but her peace is fleeting.

Fear suddenly seizes her like a physical grip on the back of her head and she is a little girl again in Ireland running with her mother across the fields in Cork, escaping from hell.

"The fear goes in through the back of my head. We are running, running all the time across the fields." Mary Collins is just 2½, but she can sense her mother's desperation.

"She was escaping. She'd found me, maybe she was looking for my sister Angela too. It could be days or weeks. I remember the rain all the time and the running."

Mary Collins pauses, before firmly choosing her words. "They captured her. That's really what it was. She needed help. They took her in. Then they captured her. They told me she was dirty, they taught me to hate her. I suffered every day because of her. I blamed her."

Forty-five years later Mary Collins wrote a poem about that hatred. But by then, she had uncovered many of the dark secrets of her mother's life and of her own, and the hatred had begun to turn to compassion and one day even to love. That day Mary Collins found herself praying to her mother for her own son's recovery from a near-fatal illness at the age of 16.

"He'd had a bone marrow transplant in King's College and then he had to have emergency surgery in Guy's Hospital for a tumour at the back of his nose. They said he could die in it. I was in a church somewhere near Guy's and I was asking her to save him. It was when I nearly lost my son that I began to feel about her. Her children had been taken from her; she had lost her three children. Two miracles happened. My son survived and I found my mother. The hatred they'd beaten into me, the shame about my family, was leaving me."

By now, Mary Collins, a 54-year-old mother of three, has begun to understand much about her mother's life and her own. But she is still haunted by fear, sometimes by anger. "It's like a shadow over me, a blackness that never goes away. I try to detach myself from it, connect to reality and do what I have to do each day. I have to for my children." And for her job. "I'm afraid anyone will find out my background. I can't tell them about my life. When I go to my kids' schools, it's the same. I'm on my own. They've no cousins, no aunts or uncles. I have two lives, but I only speak about one.

"When the Ryan Report by the Irish Government came out, it was all over the UK papers here and the TV. People in my job were talking about it. It was my life, but I couldn't speak about it."

Now she has begun to feel freer about revealing her secrets, her suffering. "I have to. My children don't ask much now but they will want to know." Two things will help her healing. Now she has become strong enough to demand that these two things happen.

"I want the people who abused brought to justice (she names one person in particular whom she believes is now living in the US). And I want the Irish Government to acknowledge how the Magdalene laundries destroyed families."

The laundries were run by four congregations: the Sisters of Our Lady of Charity, the Religious Sisters of Charity, the Sisters of Mercy and the Good Shepherd Sisters.

Mary Collins was part of a delegation that met then Justice Minister Alan Shatter in September 2011 as part of an examination of State involvement with the Magdalene Laundries that was chaired by former Senator Dr. Martin McAleese.

Mary personally told the Minister what had happened to her mother and to her sister and herself and presented him with a file of information before returning to London. "For the first time I felt some sense of relief. I gave him the proof. I put it on the table."

Two years later, Mary Collins made a return trip to Dublin as news spread that, following the McAleese report, the Taoiseach would make a formal apology for the suffering endured by women like Mary's mother, incarcerated in the laundries, many until they died there.

Well over a year earlier, a former Sister of Mercy used the term "Dante's inferno" to describe the laundries to a nationwide audience on RTÉ's *News at One* programme. Recalling a week she spent as a novice at a laundry in Galway run by the order, Patricia Burke Brogan told listeners:

"I felt I was in Dante's inferno with what I saw. It was a room full of machines and women and the women seemed to merge into the machines, the greyness, the steam, the sweating walls. I was their jailor, really."

At the age of seven Mary Collins saw her mother in a similar laundry, run by the Religious Sisters of Charity at Peacock Lane in Cork, and has carried the nightmare with her ever since.

"I saw how broken these women were. The Home they put me in made one mistake. Usually the mothers had no contact with their children; families were split up. But at the age of seven, I was brought from the Home to see my mother in the laundry. I remember that. I'm carrying her life there with me all the time. I won't forget."

She hasn't forgotten. Eleven years ago, Mary Collins travelled with her three children, Craig, Laura and Anthony, from London to Cork to find her mother's grave. She was anguished to discover that the grave in which her mother had been buried was a large communal plot in St Finbarre's Cemetery, outside the city.

On a tall wide headstone above the communal grave, the Religious Sisters of Charity had listed 72 names of women who had worked in the Peacock Lane laundry and who had died there in the 67 years between 1930 and 1997.

Next to the names of the 72 women was listed one detail only – their date of death.

The 69th name on the headstone read "Angela Collins 27.1.1988."

"When we were at the grave, my son said 'when I'm big I'll put flowers on my Nan's grave.' I think it was only then I really realised she was a grandmother too."

Today, Mary Collins has erected a separate memorial plaque in the shape of a heart, marking the grave where her mother rests. It reads:

*ANGELA COLLINS / St.Vincent's, Peacock Lane, Cork / Suffering
Lifelong Separation / From her Children / Until her death in 1988 / On
the feast of St Angela / Aged 57 years / Now at peace / In her eternal
Home / RIP"*

Mary Collins, a practising Catholic, found a degree of comfort in the realization that her mother had died on the feast day of St. Angela, and was moved further when the Ursuline Order, which had been founded by St Angela, presented the family with a statue of the saint at a memorial Mass.

At that memorial Mass to bless the graveside plaque, on January 27, 2003, 15 years after her mother's death, Mary Collins said: "From this day on, Angela is acknowledged as the unique person she was in her life, and her grandchildren have a 'Nan' to carry in their hearts."

It will be a dignified place for her children to remember their grandmother. But in remembering her life, it would be easy for them to feel angry about what happened to their grandmother and to their mother.

Angela Collins was the mother of three daughters. Mary, born in 1960 in Caherciveen, Co. Kerry, was the middle girl. Angela, the eldest, was born in 1948 in Tralee, Co. Kerry. Their youngest sister Margaret was born in 1962 in Mallow, Co, Cork. The three girls all had the same father, Patrick Collins, but he and their mother were not married. "We might have been different but were still a family unit and we were well looked after."

As a grown woman in London years later, Mary Collins discovered the family was different in another way, too. "It came as a terrible shock. I felt so ashamed. I was always afraid anyone would find out."

Now, partly through the tragedies in her own life, she has begun to come to terms with her family history. "It explains a lot, why they hated me so much, made me hate my mother, my sister too. The other girls were beaten but they were vicious to me."

Sitting on a seat by the Thames Embankment, Mary Collins is barely aware that clouds have covered the sun and a soft rain has begun to fall. She is looking down at a piece of paper on her lap. "It's something I've never told anyone before. I can tell it now," she says, lifting her head and straightening her shoulders.

"It's there," she said. "There it is." It is a page of headed notepaper from the Cork branch of The Irish Society for the Prevention of Cruelty to Children. In it, Mary Collins has crossed out two words. They appear to be the same word and then they become decipherable immediately she says them, quietly once, then firmly, proudly, the second time.

"Itinerant, itinerant. I crossed it out; I hated the word. I was ashamed. But I'm not ashamed anymore. It's all of them who should be ashamed, the Irish Government too. What happened to us, to my mother, my sister, I think it was worse because we were Travellers."

Mary Collins calls her story "explosive" because she believes it shows the role of agencies of the State in "capturing Travellers as labour for these institutions." Certainly, her story is a rare insight into the destruction of one Traveller family and its tragic aftermath. Documentation confirms Mary Collins' family background but she does not wish to publicly name any other Traveller family, to protect their privacy.

We do not know, over the long history of abuse within religious-run institutions in Ireland, how many other Travellers might have suffered like Mary Collins and her family. But in recent decades, a notorious case involving abuse of young Travellers came to light, this time at a residential home in Co. Wicklow.

Trudder House was set up in 1975 by a voluntary group, Dublin Committee for Travelling People, for children from the Travelling community who had been involved in crime and sentenced by the courts. In August 1985, *New Hibernia* magazine reported "irregularities" at the home and allegations of beatings and homosexual child abuse.

In January 1995, a Garda Síochána investigation was launched and at least 19 former residents made allegations of sexual abuse against six people associated with the home, and a case ensued against one of them. One of the first directors of Trudder House, Duncan McInnes from Scotland, was suspected of having raped and abused dozens of children in the home. He fled the country after complaints were made in 1981 and later died in Canada.

For Mary Collins, her nightmare always begins with running. She doesn't remember that fateful day that her sister, Angela, ran away from home at the age of 14 but she does remember her mother trying to find her.

"She must have been trying to find Angela. I think Angela was always rebellious. When the guards found Angela, she was somewhere in Cork.

Then they came looking for my mother. Maybe she was afraid they'd take me too."

Looking back, Mary Collins believes that a visit from the ISPCC to their camp at Castlemartyr, near Midleton, on the morning of March 21, 1962, must have been very frightening for her mother. "By the time the ISPCC official had left he'd got her to agree he could take Angela to the Good Shepherd Convent. There was no reason to take her. He says in his report, we were all 'well nourished'. That must be what frightened my mother."

The ISPCC report on the visit makes an allegation of "neglect" against the mother but further down it confirms what Mary Collins said, describing the children, Angela and Mary, as being "well nourished". Mary Collins believes that the "real problem for the ISPCC was that we were camped on the side of the road and my mother had children without being married."

Certainly, the ISPCC inspector's report appears to be primarily concerned with the nature, rather than the condition, of the Collins family. It reads:

> *"I interviewed the Mother of the children today. She told me she was married to Patrick Collins, an itinerant and that she was expecting another baby. The girl Ann (Angela) Collins was in the county home, having run away from her mother. She agreed to let Inspector take this girl to the Good Shepherd Cork. I again had a talk with the Mother, as I was not satisfied that she was married. After some time, she admitted that she was not married. She is of low intellect. She was camped near Castlemartyr with people also of itinerant stock. The Mother of the Collins children said that the girl, Ann (Angela), was 14 yrs last September, and was born in Tralee, and was confirmed in Dungarven."*

The inspector concludes:

> *"Ann taken to the Good Shepherd Convent this evening."*

"I think she was frightened I'd be next. I think she must have set off after that with me and maybe she was looking for Angela." Mary doesn't remember how long they travelled or whether they ever got as far as the Good Shepherd Convent.

We do know that about two months later, on May 17, 1962, her sister Margaret was born near Mallow. A separate ISPCC report refers to Margaret as being "abandoned in Mallow". Mary believes, from an incident she details later, that her mother gave Margaret up for adoption under pressure.

Mary thinks that sometime over the next eight months she and her mother travelled up to her mother's family in Galway. "I know the families were very close. Traveller families are; family is everything." But by January 1963, they were back again in Cork. "She hadn't got Angela out of the convent; Margaret was gone from her; she must have been getting desperate."

Things were indeed getting desperate. On January 3, 1963, Mary's mother was found begging near Midleton County Home, where she and her daughter were "given shelter". "She hated it," she told Mary, "she was afraid they'd keep us."

One or two days later, Angela Collins ran away from Midleton County Home with Mary. "She escaped," Mary Collins says. "That sealed her fate for the rest of her life.

"She must have been trying to go back to Galway. I think she was trying to find Angela too. She didn't get Angela. She did have me.

"I remember running. It must have been winter. I remember the rain, running through the fields. Running and sodden in the rain."

But Angela Collins and her daughter never made it to Galway. We don't know how far mother and daughter travelled that sodden winter day but sometime on January 5, 1963, their bid to escape to Galway ended abruptly when they were stopped trying to board a bus for Tuam.

We learn from an ISPCC report, dated January 14, 1963, that Angela Collins "intended to travel back to Tuam with her child Mary on 5.1.63 without the necessary money for the fare to Tuam and in most inclement weather."

Then we learn how Angela Collins' fate was indeed sealed that day for the rest of her life. According to the ISPCC, the Medical Officer of Midleton Hospital "certified that this Mother was unfit to have the custody charge or care of her child and advised that the child be placed in care."

We don't know on what authority Angela Collins was sent back to Midleton County Home, but we do know that this time she returned there alone.

Angela Collins, then aged 30, was transferred soon afterwards from Midleton County Home, run by the Religious Sisters of Mercy, to St Vincent's Convent Peacock Lane Laundry in Cork city, run by the Sisters of Charity. Official documents later described her as an "inmate" at Peacock Lane.

While, again, we don't know under what, if any, legal authority Angela Collins was transferred to Peacock Lane Laundry, we do know that she would remain there for the next 27 years of her short life.

She would spend all of those 27 years working in the laundry until her death from ovarian cancer on January 27, 1988, at the age of 57.

Nine days later when the Sisters of Charity registered her death, Angela Collins was described on her death certificate as "single".

"They weren't individuals, they had no past and no present, simply worked to the end," Mary Collins says. That was why it was important to Mary Collins to mark her mother's grave with a separate plaque "to acknowledge her life as an individual. All these women were individuals. They had families. They had children."

Soon after her mother was sent back to Midleton County Home, the ISPCC sought permission to commit her daughter Mary, then aged 2½ , to Cobh Industrial School. The communication from the ISPCC, dated 14.1.63, was addressed to "Sec, Galway County Council, Galway" as follows:

Dear Sir,

Please take note that I intend to make application for the committal of the Above named child to Cobh Industrial School, at Cobh District Court, on 27.1.63 on the grounds of having a parent not exercising proper guardianship.

The mother of the child is Mary (Angela) Collins, an itinerant. The latter arrived in Cork on 3.1.63 with her child and took shelter in Midleton Co. Home, Cork. She told me that she came from the Tuam area Co. Galway. She admitted that she was not married and was cohabiting with a man, also an itinerant. She has a total of three children of the association,

Ann (Angela) Collins aged 14 yrs in the Good Shepherd Convent, Cork and Margaret Collins born the 17.5.62 and later abandoned in Mallow, Co. Cork. She intended to travel back to Tuam with her child Mary on the 5.1.63 without the necessary money for the fare to Tuam and in most inclement weather. The MO Midleton Hospital certified that this Mother was unfit to have the custody charge or care of her child and advised that the child be placed in care. The child was given shelter in Cobh Convent. The Mother is still in the County Home, Midleton. My Hon. Sec. believes that the responsibility of the child rests with Galway County Council seeing that the mother resided in that area up to 3.1.63 according to her version.

She is illiterate and obvious to anyone that she is unfit to have the care of any child.

I would be thankful for an early reply to my letter with your views etc."

We don't have the response from Galway County Council to this letter, but we do know from other documents that just one month later, on February 15, 1963, Mary Teresa Collins appeared before Cobh District Court. The court ruled that the 2½-year-old girl should be committed to a local industrial school, St Coleman's Industrial School, Rushbrook, Cobh.

She was brought there on February 27, 1963, and was designated number 5 by the religious order that ran the institution (Sisters of Mercy). "I lost my name in the home. I was just number 5."

Mary Collins would remain there for the next 15 years of her life, suffering beatings and humiliation, while all the time being taught to hate her mother. "They must have hated her because she had illegitimate children and she was a Traveller too. I was beaten because of her; they told me she was dirty. They taught me to hate her. They took her from me and then they taught me to hate her. They beat it into me."

Mary Collins doesn't remember much about the first year in the institution, but she does remember the fear from an early age, and the frequent beatings.

"My time there was full of fear. A lot of the children got beatings there. I was getting beaten because of my mother. I was beaten a lot for snoring. I would be asleep and taken from my bed and stripped naked.

They would stretch me across the table in the washroom. Pillows were put over my head and big girls held me down while I was beaten.

"There was a farm about five minutes from the home. Many a night I was beaten and taken up there. There was a pigsty there with four fat pigs. They were very smelly. I used to scream at them not to leave me there. I didn't know what I'd done, but I kept saying I'm sorry." Later in the night when all the other children were asleep, someone would come back for her. "I remember going back into the home when it was dark and getting into my bed."

In a description of her terror to a London doctor two decades later, Mary Collins spoke about hearing the latch of the pigsty closing and starting to scream. "The door would remain locked," the medical report recorded, "and she would be left there. She was afraid of the pigs and would cower in a corner."

The coal shed held terrors for her too. "I was very afraid of the black cat they had in the shed with the coal. The shed used to be full up with coal and the cat slept there. I was put in there a lot. I would scream when they put me in there. This always happened after homework or reading. I'd be slapped on the face really hard for not getting something right. It was so hard my neck would hurt. I used to go to school with scratches and bruises on my face."

On some occasions in the institution, she would break out in sores and spirits would be put on them. "Then they would get a scissors and cut each sore off my body. I was howling and begging them to stop. They told me it was the dirt in me coming out. My body was paralysed with pain. Then they wrapped me in bandages and I wore newspapers over my bandages to stop me scratching. I was locked away in the dormitory till I healed."

She could hear birds singing outside the dormitory and in this, Mary Collins found a brief measure of peace, imagining herself free like the birds from the hell around her.

"I used to watch the birds and I'd make different shapes from the trees. The birds were so calm. I used to wish I was a bird."

Amid all the trauma and the terror, one day stands out. It was the day she was taken to Peacock Lane Laundry to meet the mother she'd been taught to hate.

"I was about seven that day when a nun told me I was going to see my mother. The thought of going to see my mother scared me. I had no feelings about her. I didn't really know what a mother was. I believed it was something bad.

"I was miserable on the train to Cork. When the train stopped, we walked down the road and got a bus. We stopped at a big building with holy statues outside. A nun answered the door. Nobody talked to me. I was sent into this room with a big round table and four chairs. It had a big clock on the wall. It was very cold. It took ages for my mother to come. I sat in silence waiting for her. I could hear the heavy walking in the hallway as she came down. The door opened and it was the nun and my mother and a friend of my mother's, a Mary Ellen."

Decades later, as she read the names on the headstone over the communal grave for the dead of the laundry, Mary Collins was shocked when she reached the final name. It read "Mary Ellen Moran 19.2.1997". Mary Collins believes this was the same woman who had been in the room with her mother that day 30 years earlier.

"My mother kept her eyes on the floor and said hello in a husky voice," Mary Collins recalls. "She sat down as did Mary Ellen and nobody talked.

"My mother was staring at the table. She couldn't look at me. I didn't like the look of her eyes, they were sunk in and her movements were slow. B (name provided) from the institution was kicking me under the table. She gave me an awful look. She was saying talk to your mother. I couldn't. I didn't know how I was to talk to her, as I was never allowed to talk to adults in the institution. I was watching the clock go round and round. I sat there for a long time not understanding what I was to do or how I was to react. It was time to leave. My mother stood at the door and said goodbye. I was happy that it was over."

Her relief would be short lived. "B must have been angry I hadn't spoken during the visit. When she got me back to the home, she marched me in, hitting my head and throwing me on the ground.

"She brought me into the dressing area and stripped me naked. I was struggling when she was hitting me so she grabbed me and laid me down naked and I was screaming because she was hurting me, stretching my hand behind my back. She called the big girls to hold me down. They got pillows to put over my head so she couldn't hear my screaming. She kept telling me I was like my mother.

"I never wanted to see my mother again because I believed she had brought me such pain. I wished I was treated like the other girls who didn't have mothers. I never knew my mother in any way other than just someone I got abused over."

But there appears to have been another, even more sinister, reason for the anger and brutality that day. "I found out they wanted my mother to sign papers that day to have my sister Margaret adopted. I believe they told her if she signed them, she could see me.

"She must have signed them after that. Margaret (now Teresa) was five by then. She'd held out for five years. I think their plan was for me to be put up for adoption too. But she was too stubborn. She held out for five years with Teresa. After that, they used to bring me to see her about twice a year. They kept that side of the agreement.

"I believe now she didn't want to give any of us away, Angela or Margaret or me. They made her suffer for that.

"The one mistake they made was taking me to see her. I'll always remember that, how she looked, broken and frightened. When I was about 15, I went to visit my mother on my own. I still sat around a table and never spoke and she didn't speak. But it was different. I wasn't going to get a beating afterwards. When I saw her, I discovered later, she was all drugged up."

Thirty-five years later, at a meeting in Dublin in 2010 about the Magdalene laundries, Mary Collins was shocked to discover more details about her mother's life from a woman who had been in the laundry with her.

That woman's name is Annie Coughlin, who spent half of her life in Magdalene laundries until the age of 32. Annie, now 75 and happily married for the past 34 years, is a short, petite woman, who speaks in a gentle, firm voice.

"I was in several of the Magdalene laundries and this man asked me at the meeting if I knew anyone at St Vincent's (Peacock Lane) named Collins. I had to think and then I remembered, I said yes I knew a girl, Angela was her name. God she was a lovely poor woman. I remember as well as anything the night she came in to us.

"The reason I remember is that she was hammering down the door with the bedpan and she reminded me of myself. They used to put us in our own little room at half seven and bolt us in till the following morning and they expected you to stay there till half six the following morning. They wanted you to use the bedpan in your room. But I wouldn't use the bedpan and I used to take the bedpan up and hammer the door to let me out of the locked room because I used to be frightened there would be a fire; I used to have nightmares. Angela was like me, hammering at the door, that's why I remember her.

"When I heard the banging that morning, I had to go over to her. I didn't know who she was. And God help her, she was in a terrible state, pouring sweat. God, the poor thing was scared. I remember Mary Ellen Moran was with her and Mary Ellen said Angela was her name. God, she was sweating and sweating and I sat on the bed and rubbed her hair. Her hair was wringing wet and I was sitting on the bed and stroking her hair away from her. I don't know how long I was with her, she never said anything, and then she fell off to sleep.

"You can imagine how Angela must have suffered going in there; all her daughters taken from her. Imagine your daughters taken from you and then you were bolted in all night, I don't think I would have just banged the door; I'd be a lot worse.

"I didn't see her much. She was a very quiet woman; I never heard her voice. We all had our own jobs, our own quotas, I'd pass her and give her a pat and she'd smile, that was it. Mary Ellen was very good to her; consoling her. I think Mary Ellen felt very sorry for her. Angela was lovely looking. Mary has the two big brown eyes of Angela, the dark hair, the pale skin."

Beyond the loss, loneliness, and fear that tortured Angela Collins, she appears to have been treated reasonably well physically in Peacock Lane though she would have worked extremely hard in the laundry. "I have to say I was treated OK there," Annie Coughlin says. "I was in 10 laundries. I was in the Good Shepherds all my life till I went to St Vincent's.

"The Good Shepherds were brutal. I was in Limerick, Waterford, New Ross, Limerick again, Cork. We were only children, if you didn't get the work done, you weren't allowed into the dining room for food. If I pinched bread or for speaking in the dining room or arriving late for Mass, they'd dress me and shift me off to another laundry. You never heard anything about anyone. There were young people, mothers, I saw old people in the dining room and the flesh used to be off their fingers."

It was the mid-Sixties in the Good Shepherd in Cork, might she have come across Mary Collin's sister Angela? "I could have been there when Mary's sister was there. You never knew. You had a number, no names, you never spoke to anyone, you never knew anything about anyone." From Cork, she went to Galway and then "someone got me out of Galway and I went to St Vincent's. They said you won't be beaten here. I have to say I was treated OK and I had my name back, but we did work hard, from 8 in the morning until half six."

We can get a picture of the kind of hard, monotonous life Angela Collins must have lived each day in Peacock Lane from Annie Coughlin's description.

It all revolved around work, ceaselessly it seemed, 10 hours a day, quotas to be met, clothes to be cleaned, a seemingly endless supply, from colleges and convents it came, from hotels and guesthouses, from hospitals and homes, all adding up to quite a business, except all the women got was food to eat, a bed to sleep in, a room to be locked in.

"You got up about half six, Mass was at 7, breakfast after that, then you tidied your room and the bell went at 8 o' clock. We all had to answer the bell and go down to the laundry. You got your quota to do. Everything had to be laundered, separated, folded, sorted, from hotels, guest houses, hospitals, colleges, all different colours. You had lunch at 12.30 till about one and then worked all day long till 6.30. But we were fed well in Cork, definitely fed well there. But we never seemed to stop working. "

While her sister and mother worked hard in the institutions, Mary Collins too was "scrubbing and cleaning", though she also went to school nearby. "I'd have to get up early to scrub the floors first."

But learning brought its own terrors. "I couldn't speak properly and I couldn't pronounce my words properly," she recalls, partly due to a nasal problem that caused speech difficulties. For this she was mocked and laughed at in school, while "home" in the institution she was beaten. "When I couldn't speak properly I had my face pushed on the desk. I used to have nosebleeds. This happened nearly every day after school. I couldn't learn."

Apart from the first visit to her mother at the age of seven, and subsequently about twice a year, the only other family contact Mary had was letters from her sister Angela in the Good Shepherd Convent, the sister she had last seen when she was 2½ . But these letters, too, would become a source of suffering for her. Soon she came to dread their arrival and to hate her sister, as she had been taught to hate her mother.

"Angela used to write a lot of letters to me from the convent until she left at about 17 and went to England.

"I was very young. I don't remember much about the letters. I remember once she sent a photo of herself. They showed it to me, but then they kept it. The nuns would read the letters out loud before everyone. They'd ridicule her. They said she was stupid, that she was dirty. I hated listening to the letters. I know she used to write to my mother too"

Mary never wrote back to Angela. No replies ever came either from her mother. This enforced silence from her sister and her mother would ultimately result, as we shall see, in tragic consequences for Angela Collins.

At the age of 13, Mary remembers doing what any young girl loves to do at that age – look in a mirror. But she suffered for that too. "I was called a tramp, a bad egg and a whore like my mother. I think they were trying to make me hate my body in case I'd turn out like my mother."

As Mary Collins turned 14, in the summer of 1974, the world outside the institution was suffering its own national trauma. The country was still reeling from the Monaghan and Dublin bombings that killed 33 people at the height of the Northern Ireland conflict.

In Dublin, a young senator named Mary Robinson, who would go on to become president of Ireland 16 years later, had begun to question laws that were strongly supported by the Catholic Church but which she believed limited people's lives. That year she introduced a bill to amend the law on the sale of contraceptives, only to see it defeated.

In was the year that campaigners began to demand that the Irish state should remove the legal concept of "illegitimacy" because it denied equal rights to children born outside marriage.

It was also the year that Mary Collins tried to run away from the institution. "I remember after school when I was 14 I tried to run away, me and another girl," she recalls. They managed to get as far as Cobh.

"We went down to the pier. There was a foreign ship in. We talked to the sailors. They promised to take us away when the ship was leaving." But when the girls left Cobh that day it was not on a reckless or romantic trip aboard a foreign ship but in the back of a Garda car. "The guards turned up and found us and took us back to the home" – and into the arms of more brutality.

"Sister X (name provided) nearly killed me. She bashed my head off the iron post in the cloakroom. She told me I would have had a black baby if I went with them."

But around this time the unrelenting savagery had begun to abate, partly, Mary believes, because some lay staff left the institution. "They were as bad, if not worse than some of the nuns."

Mary would go on to complete her Inter Cert though she didn't find exams easy. Once when she failed an exam she was told she would be sent to work in the laundry. "I remember Sister X pulling my hair and telling me I was no good and I was just like my mother and she was going to see if I could go and work in the laundry with my mother. I was begging her not to do that. I was pleading with her not to send me where my mother was.

"A family I'd gone to in the summer asked for me back. They were lovely. They'd treated me like family. But the nuns lied. They said I wasn't still there. It was sheer malice and hatred. In the end they knew a woman in Cork who was looking for a cleaner and I was sent there."

Mary Collins left the institution in 1977, to take up the job and was formally discharged in 1978. She was now almost 18 years old and had spent nearly 15 years in the institution. But she wasn't to leave without a departing jibe. In her discharge report, a social worker wrote, "Mary won't make much of her life."

Soon afterwards, what seemed like a miracle happened. Mr D.E. Bowles, a London dentist, and his family walked into her life. Mary has a letter from Mr Bowles recalling what happened.

> *"In 1978 I was working in the UK as a dentist. I was on a summer holiday in Crookhaven, West Cork, with my wife and three children. It was there we befriended a family whom I recall being named McKnight. Mary was working with the family looking after their children and as I understood, was with them for the summer.*
>
> *"It was through the McKnight family that we were recommended to visit the Home. Myself and my wife visited the home and enquired about employing Mary to care for our children back in the UK.*
>
> *"Mary was discharged on 15.7.1978 and I became her legal guardian."*

Mary Collins formal discharge from the institution states she was discharged, after doing her Inter Cert, on 15/07/1978 "to train as a dental nurse by Dr. E. Bowles," It noted Dr. Bowles UK address and added: "Dr. Bowles is from near Cork and is known to the school." It also stated, "Mother has no fixed abode. Presently an inmate of St Vincent's Convent Peacock Lane, Cork."

Mary points out that contrary to what the discharge record says about her training to be a dental nurse, there was no such agreement between herself and Dr. Bowles. "That wasn't the case. I went to work as a domestic in Mr Bowles' house, not as a dental assistant but to help with the children."

Mary moved to London with Mr Bowles and his family and by all accounts, it was a very good time in her life. The family was good to her and she felt happy with them. It was not to last long, however. About two years later, the Bowles' marriage broke up and Mary Collins went back to Ireland, where the Bowles' had helped to find her another job with a Cork family.

She visited her mother again in Peacock Lane and still found she hardly spoke and looked very depressed. "Once I asked Sr. M about my mother and how they treated her. She told me when my mother came in she tried to "smash the place up" to get out, so they had to sedate her. I think she was drugged up all the time to stop her getting out. Mary Ellen said that too. The nuns wouldn't tell me anything else about her.

"I did find out the name of a doctor treating her in Cork and I went to see him. He just said she was being treated well but he wouldn't tell me anything more than that."

Life back in Ireland, however, wasn't working out for Mary Collins. "I hit lows. There were too many bad memories." Soon she found herself homeless. "A woman I knew took me in. I had no money, no unemployment benefits or anything. I was nobody."

"Teresa somehow found out about it and sent over my fare to London." But the sisters were strangers to one another. After over two decades apart, it was hardly surprising.

Mary stayed in a room in Teresa's flat but they didn't get along. "We were fighting all the time over my mother. Maybe envy, jealousy. I'd been kept, she hadn't. One day when I came back from work, she asked me to leave. I ended up homeless."

We know now that this was the fate of large numbers of survivors of institutional abuse. They tried to escape from Ireland to make a new life in England but they often ended up on the streets of London or Liverpool or other cities, alone, destitute and forgotten.

Mary's life now seemed headed that way. She ended up living in squats in the city for most of the next five years. Then her life suddenly changed.

At the age of 27, Mary met a man with whom she fell in love, and who became her partner. A year later, her mother died. She travelled to Ireland with her sister Teresa for her mother's funeral. "I was glad she was dead. I still hated her then but eventually I decided to travel over for the funeral."

Over the next two decades, Mary and her partner had three children together. But their relationship wasn't working and they finally decided to split up over a decade ago.

Mary Collins' children, born in 1991, 1993 and 1996, are the anchors of her life. She is also proud of the fact that they have been excelling in their exams. She has worked hard in London and is now manager in a community services centre. Clearly, she has made a good life for her children and for herself. Yet, beneath the surface, she is suffering every day.

"It's like a black shadow over me all the time." A medical report describes how she has nightmares of being stranded and of things happening to her children and that she frequently wakes up crying at night. She also suffers from panic attacks. She has attended clinics at Guy's Hospital and the Maudsley Hospital and these sessions have helped her to overcome the severity of her depression.

"But the black shadow is always there, the flashbacks, the nightmares. They come quietly, sometimes. I'm watching television and there's a violent scene and I have to turn it off. The pain is always there, just below the surface."

Like the pain she felt last year, when she switched on the TV and Sky was showing scenes of jubilation in Rome, after the election of Pope Francis.

"I watched the processions and everyone looked happy and I thought about the processions in the Home for some church holiday. We'd all march in the town, the priests in their robes, everyone dressed up and everyone would look happy, and then we'd go back to the abuse. Looking at the celebrations for the Pope reminded me of that, that hidden world, it was very upsetting.

"He says he's sorry, but what's the meaning of sorry if people have answered to no-one, if someone hasn't been brought to justice.

"Someone is responsible for my sister's life and for my mother's life but no-one is accountable. If they're not accountable now our children will want to know why, why these things happened to their parents or grandparents and no-one was brought to justice."

Ten years after Mary Collins had made the journey to Cork to erect a memorial plaque to honour her mother, she was back in Ireland again, sitting next to Aislinn Centre founders Christine Buckley and Carmel McDonnell-Byrne, in the packed public gallery of Dáil Éireann.

As 7pm approached, on February 19, 2013, the Taoiseach entered the chamber. There was absolute silence. Many sensed that tonight the nation would finally acknowledge the cruelty inflicted in 10 laundries on the 10,000 Magdalene women, most of whom, like Mary's mother, had long since died, never knowing this night might come.

As the Taoiseach began to speak, Mary Collins shuddered. He was talking of dark secrets, of cruel and pitiless times.

"What we address today is how you took this country's terrible 'secret' and made it your own. Burying it, carrying it in your hearts here at home, or with you to England and to Canada, America and Australia, on behalf of Ireland and the Irish people. But from this moment on you need carry it no more," he said, glancing upwards at the gallery where Mary Collins and the other women sat.

"I believe I speak for millions of Irish people all over the world when I say we put away these women because for too many years we put away our conscience. We swapped our personal scruples for a solid public apparatus that kept us in tune and in step with a sense of what was 'proper behaviour' or the 'appropriate view' according to a sort of moral code that was fostered at the time particularly in the 1930s, 40s and 50s. We lived with the damaging idea that what was desirable and acceptable in the eyes of the Church and the State was the same and interchangeable."

"This," he told the women *"was a cruel, pitiless Ireland distinctly lacking in a quality of mercy."*

The Magdalene Women might have been told that they were washing away a wrong or a sin, he said: *"but we know now and to our shame they were only ever scrubbing away our nation's shadow. Today, just as the State accepts its direct involvement in the Magdalene Laundries, society too has its responsibility."*

As most of the nation watched on television and many Irish abroad logged on to their computers, the Taoiseach said: *"I believe I speak for millions of Irish people all over the world when I say we put away these women because for too many years we put away our conscience."*

Then the Taoiseach looked up again at the gallery. Words that Mary Collins never believed she would ever hear from anyone in Ireland, never mind the leader of an Irish Government, now fell upon a hushed chamber.

"The perception that the Magdalene Laundries were reserved for what were offensively and judgementally called "fallen women" is not based upon fact at all but upon prejudice. The women are and always were wholly blameless. Therefore, I, as Taoiseach, on behalf of the State, the Government and our citizens deeply regret and apologise unreservedly to all those women for the hurt that was done to them, and for any stigma they suffered, as a result of the time they spent in a Magdalene Laundry."

Looking down, Mary Collins quietly wept.

She was thinking of her mother, her sister. She was also thinking of her daughter, watching in London, and of her granddaughter Angel Mary.

A mixture of emotions overwhelmed her.

"As I sat in the Dáil, I was crying my heart out. As he spoke, I felt 'my Mum is a person tonight'. That was the connection I felt. My Mum was a person again. She was nobody in life, not to be spoken about. It was an acknowledgement of her. She was part of Ireland now.

"I think I was feeling differently from the other women. They were happy. Things he was saying like that nobody believed them; they did the dirty washing for Ireland all these years. But I was thinking about her life, that she wasn't part of anybody's life, she wasn't part of life at all.

"She wasn't to be spoken about, you live your life, you get on with your life but there was this dark horror all the time, you don't mention her, now I felt all of Ireland was listening about these women, about my mother.

"In the Dáil, all of a sudden, she became part of life."

But at the same time that the apology connected Mary with her mother, it also severed them, she felt, isolating her from her mother's suffering, not acknowledging the family connection.

"Although I was surrounded by people, I felt alone. I felt that my suffering hadn't been acknowledged. I felt that although my Mum became a person that night, I also felt alone. I was like a little girl again going up to the laundry, a big laundry with all these women. I felt I was cut off from my Mum as a child. She was taken away from me and they made me hate her but that night in the Dáil, I felt I was cut off from her because we weren't connected together. He (the Taoiseach) didn't connect me to what was going on. There was no mention of her family; he could have mentioned the children of the women, apologised to them too. Not many of the women are alive, not many of their children are out there anymore, and he should have mentioned their children. They were mothers with families, many of them. But he never spoke about their children.

"At one stage I felt I didn't want to leave the Dáil until I had the answer to why, why her children were not included in this apology. I'm happy for the (Magdalene) women but not fully happy myself, for me it's unfinished.

"Before all this came out, for years, for 20 years, I had been the one fighting for my mother. The Government really prolonged the suffering, knowing I had those records all those years and they never, ever believed me. Now I have an apology and an admission they were enslaved into the laundries. That's the big difference now – the whole world knows what I've always known."

ANGELA COLLINS

Liverpool, once described as resembling a city in a gloomy Victorian novel, must have seemed a cold place even in the 60s as the ships pulled in from Dublin, carrying their cargo of homesick Irish.

But, like the generations before them, these Irish slowly began to settle in. They got to know the city better; it was the era of the Beatles and, for some, there was an aura of excitement. Soon it became less intimidating, less lonely and in time many would make the city their home.

But for others, like Angela Collins, Liverpool would never be home. Their thoughts were nearly always somewhere in Ireland. We don't know what thoughts were running through Angela Collins' mind as Christmas Day approached in 1977, but possibly, she was thinking about her arrival in the city exactly 10 years earlier when she was just 19.

She may have been thinking too of her sister Mary and of her mother, because we know from her letters to them in the past that she has often thought about them. Mary would be nearly 17 by now, her mother probably in her late 40s. Angela may be hoping for a card or a letter from them, maybe finally this Christmas the silence would be broken.

She may have noticed how splendid the city looked, ablaze with lights and Christmas colour. But she was more likely to have been thinking of other Christmases long past, in other places, maybe Tuam, maybe Mallow, maybe that last Christmas in Midleton in 1961 or was it '62, we're not sure which one, but we know from her sister, Mary, that Christmastime held a special magic for the family.

It was never the presents, there were never many of those. It was the warmth of the big fire, everyone gathered round and the smell of something special cooking. There was Mass in the morning, scurrying home before everyone else left the church, back to the campfire, sitting round it together, the warmth on their hands and their faces, the sparks like souls going up to Heaven, her mother said. That was a special Christmas. It was the last Christmas before Angela ran away.

Angela was always like that, testing the waters, too rebellious for her own good, 14 then, the big sister. Wasn't that the Christmas it all began to change. From then on, nothing would ever be the same for any of them. Had she made them all suffer, had she caused it all. Maybe that was it. That was why they hadn't written: maybe they blamed her. If she'd stayed there, things might have been OK for them. But she hadn't stayed and when Christmas Day passed that year and the light of the morning came, she was gone.

It was OK for a while, some farmers' wives were nice and gave her food; others hunted her away. But then January came and with it the rain and in a week she was feeling too cold and wet and hungry to keep going.

Then she came to a village and the guards saw her begging; they told her they were going to find her mother and they were going to take her back to her.

She may be remembering arriving at the camp, somewhere in Cork, and the guards admonishing her mother because she'd let her run away. They came back again another time, maybe a few days day later, and this time they had another man with them.

The guards were watching her playing outside with Mary, and inside was that other man. Perhaps she could hear her mother raising her voice and the man's loud voice and then her mother was quiet, or did she hear her crying? And the man coming out and before she knew what was going on, she was put in the back of the car.

She's desperately trying to remember them, her mother and Mary, but their faces keep eluding her. That was the worst part. She'd had nothing to carry with her all these years. Except that Christmas, that time before everything changed and she lost them.

She had tried over the years in the Good Shepherd Convent in Cork to keep in touch with them. She knew her mother was in the laundry at Peacock Lane and that Mary was in Cobh. She'd written to them from the convent often; that was the one thing she was able to do there.

She'd always been good about the letters: for nearly three years, from the time she went in at 14, lots of letters. Once she'd even sent a photo to Mary, but why hadn't they ever written back? Mary was very small, of course, she was only five or six then. But nothing from her mother either, not a line. How many Christmases had passed since then, nine of them here and now another one to pass?

Some may have gone mercifully quickly, her sister Mary hopes, in a haze of wine or too much beer because she knows Angela sometimes drank a lot.

But it numbed the loneliness, stilled the nightmares. They would come in on her, probably in black, like they did for Mary, with nowhere to hide, closing in and the fear gripping her body like an iron vice. "She was only three years in the Good Shepherd but locked away like that, it must have killed her," Mary says.

Mary was only 2½ that year they'd put them all away, separated in different places. So quickly it had happened, 15 years ago now, Angela herself, her mother, Mary, maybe Margaret too. Angela never knew Margaret. She'd been born about a year after Mary. Margaret could be anyone, anywhere this Christmas. But Mary would surely still be in Cork, her mother too.

But where were they when she tried to visit them? Was she crazy to even try? It had been a long journey from Liverpool, one of the wettest winters in Ireland, then travelling all the way to Cork, to Peacock Lane, to Cobh. But no matter how crazy, she knew she had to make this journey. She had to do it now, to find them, to finally see their faces again. Then she could go back to Liverpool and everything might be a bit more bearable, the blackness would surely pass, the loneliness would ease.

But it didn't happen like that for Angela Collins. She had come back from Cork with nothing that wet winter of 1977.

They had stopped her at the gate at Peacock Lane. We know she got all the way to the gate. But then no further, they insisted. Still afraid to challenge them, still that lingering fear of authority, until finally she just gave up. Why wouldn't they let her in to see her mother, what was wrong with her mother and where had Mary gone, no sign of her either at Cobh.

Then the long journey back to Dublin, time to think, time to torment her mind. Were they even alive? And then the longer journey from Dublin to Liverpool, with nothing. She'd never heard from them and now she must have begun to believe she would never see them.

Why was there never a word, all those years and all those letters; they must have arrived safely, surely they had.

We know that all of Angela Collins' letters from the God Shepherd convent had indeed arrived safely. We are certain of that because each one was read aloud to Mary in Cobh when they arrived. But none of them had been welcome. Rather, Mary Collins had come to dread their arrival.

"The nun would read them out loud, laugh at them, make fun of her, how she couldn't write properly, in front of the whole class. I hated getting the letters, I hated my sister for writing them, they taught me to hate her, and I did.

"Anyway, I hardly knew who she was, what a sister was. The last time I saw her I was 2½. The nuns kept telling me she was bad, like my mother, she was dirty. I suppose we were all dirty to them. To be illegitimate was a sin, to be a Traveller must have been worse."

Today, Mary Collins remembers little from those letters except the humiliation she felt, was made to feel. But she does remember one thing clearly.

"One day Angela sent me a photo of herself. The nun showed it to me, I remember that, but they kept it. I never saw it again."

The letters had landed safely, too, at the laundry at Peacock Lane, but her mother was never allowed to write back, she would tell Mary later. "They didn't want her to have any contact with my sister, Mary Ellen Moran said, because they were afraid she'd run away again."

And so Angela Collins' letters to her sister and to her mother were never answered. They were never even acknowledged.

"There was no contact from me or my mother. No acknowledgement. In the end, she just stopped writing. The letters stopped when she left the Good Shepherd. Then she went to an aunt in Waterford and soon after that at about 19 she went with some others to Liverpool."

But if Angela Collins had stopped writing to her mother and to her sister, she had not stopped thinking about them in Liverpool. "I found out later from my mother that she came over and tried to find us. I don't know what they told her but my mother said she wasn't allowed in. When she came to see me in Cobh, I'd left by then. I knew nothing about it until much later."

Mary Collins had been officially discharged from Cobh in the summer of 1977 and had later left for London, with Dr. Bowles and his family. Angela Collins must therefore have travelled from Liverpool to Cork in search of her mother and her sister sometime in the winter of 1977, and had missed her sister by just a few months.

Mary Collins believes that by the time Angela left Ireland that winter the idea must have begun to take hold that her mother and sister must surely be dead. That's why they wouldn't let her see them. They must be dead. That was why they hadn't written to her.

"The despair she must have felt on the journey from Ireland probably tormented her all that winter in Liverpool," Mary Collins believes.

In the weeks that followed, that despair would deepen. No one knows what pain Angela Collins felt; we can never know that. But we do know from what followed that hope soon deserted Angela Collins until finally she lost her will to live. By Christmas, hers had become a life beyond endurance.

On Christmas Day 1977, Angela Collins died by suicide. She was just 29 years old.

It must be emphasised again that we cannot know what Angela Collins truly felt that day or in the days and months and years before that tragic event. Mary Collins can only try to piece her sister's life together, as this story has tried to do, from the fragments she has gathered over the years.

But from these she believes it was the enforced separation from her family in her childhood and later the belief they were dead that finally killed her sister. "Finally I think she just gave up hope."

"The nuns never told her we were dead," Mary Collins emphasises. "They didn't do that," she repeats firmly. "But they always made sure she'd no contact with us, not with the letters and not when she came to find us the year she died."

Mary Collins learned of her sister's death two days after Christmas Day in 1977 when she visited her mother at Peacock Lane. "The nun (whom she names) told me my mother was feeling very lonely that day because she'd just heard the news.

"Your sister's dead, Mary," the nun said.

"We've got to pay for her funeral."

"I'll always remember that. 'Your sister's dead, Mary. We've got to pay for her funeral.'"

The Religious Sisters of Charity learned about Angela Collins' death when the authorities in Liverpool contacted them. They explained that they had found the address of Peacock Lane laundry on Angela.

"We didn't get any details, just that she took her own life on Christmas Day," Mary Collins says. Neither Mary nor her mother travelled to Liverpool for Angela's funeral, though some of the extended family did.

"My mother wasn't able to go and she didn't even want to talk about it. Now I'm full of remorse, guilt, the whole lot, but then I really had no feelings for her.

"She was the sister I'd been thought to hate, the sister they'd stolen from me."

✝

For Angela Collins and others from the institutions who died by suicide, their childhood had been stolen, their will to survive damaged beyond repair. Under *Alcohol, substance abuse and self-harm*, the Ryan Commission report says the following:

> *"Four hundred and seven (407) witnesses (51%) spoke about their own suicidal thoughts and/or attempts and the death by suicide of their friends and siblings. Forty three (43) of the 407 witnesses who reported a history of suicidal thoughts also reported having made one or more suicide attempts. A further five witnesses, three male and two female, reported episodes of ongoing self-harm. One witness stated that 17 of the 39 co-residents in his class photograph had committed suicide over the years since they were discharged. Many others said they were prompted to speak to the Committee on behalf of a sibling or friend who had died by suicide and who shared the witnesses' childhood experience of abuse in institutions."*

2

STORY OF JULIE COONEY

"Horrific as the rape was, the unrelenting savagery was worse"

A little girl of four is led into a courtroom by strangers. As she enters, she sees the face of her mother, the only person she knows in the room. The little girl instinctively reaches out for her mother, but she is pulled back. They never touch. They never speak. Soon the little girl is led away from the court and it will be 10 years before Julie Cooney sees her mother again.

Julie's father died of TB at the age of 40 in 1952, when Julie was just three years old. Her only memory of him is on his deathbed. "My image as a baby, a three year old, is of someone in a bed with a white sheet."

Julie and her two brothers, Thomas aged two and Tony just one, were soon split up. In April 1953, Julie was taken to the Sisters of Mercy in Goldenbridge in Dublin and it was from there that she arrived in the courtroom.

"I have no memory at all of being taken from home, but I do remember going to court. I remember being in front of a judge with somebody from Goldenbridge.

"My mother is in the courtroom, she is sitting there, she is sitting to my right. I'm in a different area and I spot her but I'm not allowed to go near her. I'm reaching out for her but she's not coming to me and I'm being torn back from her and then I remember the judge saying I had to stay in Goldenbridge until I was 16."

Julie Cooney was led away without being allowed to speak to her mother and remembers being brought back to Goldenbridge in a black police van.

She believes her two brothers would have had to be in the courtroom, too, the same day but she has no memory of them being there. She found out later that they had been sent to St Kyran's Industrial School for Junior Boys in Rathdrum, Co. Wicklow, and later to Artane Industrial School for Senior Boys in Dublin.

The three siblings grew up as strangers and when they met again after her brothers left Artane years later there was no bond between them but she remembers buying Tony clothes when he left Artane.

By then she was working as a cleaner for a doctor's family and living in. Her brothers lived in hostels in the city and got odd jobs. Thomas went to England in the late 60s and joined the British Army. Later he left the army because he didn't want to serve in Belfast. Then he worked as a barber, got married and later divorced.

Tony married also but his marriage didn't work out either. Marriage breakdown was not uncommon among survivors. Trust had been broken in their lives, there was the inability to bond and many suffered from alcoholism or drug addiction or ended up in abusive relationships. Others, like Julie's brothers, suffered untimely deaths.

Both of Julie Cooney's brothers died when they were only in their 40s and 50s, and she believes what happened to them in Rathdrum and Artane contributed to their untimely deaths.

"They had to deal with a lot of trauma; it must have contributed. Their problems became addiction, alcoholism."

But, like many survivors, they never spoke about the trauma that blighted their adult lives as it had their childhood. "You could talk to them, especially Tommy, about anything but not that," Julie Cooney says.

Trauma and pain had been constants in her own life too, in Goldenbridge.

Like the beating she got after her First Communion in May 1956 when she was seven because a buckle had come off one of her shoes.

"I had a pair of black patent shoes. The shoes were only used by girls on the day of their First Communion and then they were left back. The thread had come out of the buckle of my shoe. On Monday morning I was asked if I'd worn the shoe and I was beaten on the hand with a stick in front of the 6th class."

Making your First Communion in Goldenbridge also meant for the Sisters of Mercy that you were now big enough to start making rosary beads.

"I remember we started making rosary beads after we'd made our First Communion. From the age of seven onwards we had to make the rosary beads after school from 3.30 until 6pm and then after tea to bedtime.

"We used wire, pliers and beads to make a dozen sets of rosary beads in this time. The rosary beads had 60 decades (10 beads in each decade) plus 12 threes. We made these every day Monday to Saturday. On Saturdays we had a half-day but we had to make a dozen and a half on Saturday morning."

It was excruciating work for small fingers. The children made the decades of the rosary by putting the beads on lengths of wire. After each bead was positioned, the wire had to be looped and cut using pliers, and each bead then had to be attached to the next bead until all 10 beads were completed.

"You had little pliers and wire and the wire was constantly digging into your skin and you just couldn't work fast enough to reach the quota every day. We were lined up every night, those who hadn't reached the quota and beaten," the Ryan Report quotes one Goldenbridge survivor as saying. Julie Cooney nods in agreement.

> *"A high level of physical abuse was perpetrated by some religious and lay staff in Goldenbridge," the Ryan Report states. "The method of inflicting punishments and the implements used were cruel and excessive and physical punishment was an immediate response to even minor infractions. Children were in constant fear of beatings and in many cases were beaten for no apparent reason. A feature of this school was a rosary bead industry that was operated from the school. This industry was conducted in a way that imposed impossible standards on children and caused great suffering to many of them. It was a school that was characterised by a regime of extreme drudgery, both in terms of the rosary bead making and the daily workload of the children."*

The Ryan Report also noted that the money made from bead making was considerable. "The best estimates as to the earnings are that an income of approximately £50 per week was achieved by this activity," it said. This would mean that over a 20-year period, from the late 1940s or early 1950s when it began until the 1960s, the Sisters of Mercy would have made in the region of £50,000. The Research Division of the Irish Central Bank, in response to a query for this book, said: "The modern value of £50,000 sterling from 1965 would approximate to €1,044,607."

It should be remembered too that such work was carried out by the children against a background not only of fear but of constant hunger. Julie Cooney recalls: "Between one and two o'clock every day I stood with other children in the yard waiting for scraps to be thrown out to us to eat."

But even worse than the hunger was the thirst. Julie recalls it matter-of-factly now, over 50 years later, but the image that comes to mind is of prison camp conditions.

The constant thirst, she says, drove her to drink water from the toilet cistern or even from the toilet bowl itself. "I used the bowl when the cistern was too high up. If you're thirsty, you drink, if you're really hungry, you steal. I remember eating out of the rabbit's cage, there was raw bread, and cabbage or lettuce leaves."

The cruelty she suffered or witnessed was usually at the hands of Sisters of Mercy but sometimes it was at the hands of lay staff.

In one harrowing incident when she was about eight she says she saw a lay worker put a girl of about four into a tumble drier. "I can't say whether it was turned on or not but I clearly remember her being put into the drier," she says, naming both the lay worker and the girl involved. "I don't know whether she (the lay worker) closed the door.

"It frightened the life out of us but we could do nothing about it. The girl was younger than me; I was about eight. It is horrific but you're protecting yourself and hoping it won't be you. You're horrified but what can you do as a child." When Julie Cooney first spoke about this incident publicly, the Sisters of Mercy denied it happened. "These lies really got to me," she says.

"In my opinion some of them got pleasure out of that, out of a child crying. They'd also put a child on a goat's back. That was terrifying for a child, they screamed in terror. What kind of adults do that? Where do they come from? They weren't nuns, they were lay teachers. They could obviously do what they liked. It was closed to the public; few got beyond the front door."

She remembers at the age of seven seeing how one girl suffered (name supplied) when she couldn't do a sum on a blackboard.

"She was older than me. She was standing at the blackboard trying to do a sum and she couldn't do it. The nun (whom she names) struck the girl on the back of the head with a stick. She collapsed on the floor of the classroom. She was then carried out of the room and brought to hospital." By the time she got back from hospital, Julie said, the nuns had circulated the rumour that the girl had struck her head off the rostrum.

She also witnessed another girl getting 55 slaps. "I counted them. I think I was 10 or 11 at the time." She saw children held down by other girls on the orders of one nun who then beat the children with a stick.

One witness in the Ryan Report described such violence by one nun thus:

> *"When you knew for sure she was arriving, there would be pushing and shoving about who was going first. Honest to God this is terrible, there would be younger children than you and you would be pushing them to get them to take the beating first. You didn't want to be the one to get the first of the strength. I am sorry, it was horrible, you had to do what you had to do. The screaming of children, the screaming of children will stay with me for the rest of my life about Goldenbridge. I still hear it; I still haven't recovered from that. Children crying and screaming, it was just endless, it never stopped for years in that place."*

Most of the beatings took place on the stairs landing outside the nun's cell late at night after the children had waited there for hours, Julie Cooney says. "She would go into her cell and get her stick. It was always the same stick, a shiny, dark wood stick with smooth edges.

On the landing, you could get between 12 and 20 slaps each. If you drew back your hand, she would hit you under the elbow with the stick to straighten your hand. You would get a feeling of an electric shock in your arm when you were hit on the elbow or the hand. She raised the stick high above her head each time she hit us.

"I dreaded these night rituals. It wasn't unusual to wait two or three hours until we heard her coming up the stairs. The older girls would push the younger ones to the front and some tried to reduce the pain by licking their hands or smearing them with floor polish. The landing beatings went on from when I was seven. I often wished I was dead or in hell.

"We were beaten for things no child in the world should ever have been beaten for, such as talking in the dormitory, not noticing the hem of your dress had come down. Often we never knew what we had done wrong.

"No-one knew what went on behind those high walls in Goldenbridge. The walls were so high in the yard that they blocked out the sun, so our lives were filled with darkness.

"We were never hugged or kissed and we were addressed by numbers. I was number 161. Even the little toddlers did not escape the abuse. They were placed on potties and sometimes strapped down."

Then, one autumn day when she was about 11, Julie Cooney would suffer one of the most brutal traumas in a girl's life.

"I was approximately 11 when I was raped. The rape happened in a single bed off the dormitories in Goldenbridge.

"It must have been autumn because I remember (she names the lay worker) bringing apples from the convent orchard.

"I remember this day he came to fix cord in the windows as the window kept slipping down. I was holding up the window for him. He closed the door and he worked on the window. After a while he started to fondle my thigh and then I remember being on the bed. He pulled down my pants and he had his own pants down. I didn't understand what was going on at the time but I know he did have full intercourse with me because I bled afterwards. I remember feeling very sticky. He told me he wasn't going to hurt me. I remember telling him he was hurting me."

There was no-one Julie Cooney could turn to in Goldenbridge in the aftermath of this horror, no one she could trust. And even if anyone believed her, she felt she was the one who would face retribution. "I didn't report it to anybody in the school because I didn't want to be sent to a reformatory school until I was 21. This threat was often used against us."

Julie Cooney was in her late 40s in April 1996 when she walked into a Garda station in Co. Waterford and made a statement about the rape.

She found the courage to do so after taking part, with Christine Buckley and other survivors, in the *Dear Daughter* documentary, shown on RTÉ in February 1996, which detailed the abuses perpetrated against children in Goldenbridge.

The stories of abuse in Goldenbridge had first entered the public domain four years earlier on RTÉ Radio 1 when Gay Byrne interviewed Christine Buckley on November 8, 1992. But it was the *Dear Daughter* documentary that finally ignited the revulsion of viewers.

Soon, other survivors began to break their silence. The litany of abuse finally led to an apology by An Taoiseach on behalf of the nation on May 11, 1999 and the setting up the same year of the Commission to Inquire into Child abuse, which lasted a decade but which finally vindicated survivors and convulsed the nation when it issued its landmark report on May 20, 2009.

But 50 years earlier when 11-year-old Julie Cooney was raped within the confines of Goldenbridge, all the little girl knew was absolute fear. It is chilling then to hear her say that, horrific as the rape was, the pervasive cruelty at Goldenbridge was even worse.

"The rape was horrific and being so young. But that was once-off, it never happened again. But these other things were on a daily basis. The hardest thing is the lack of respect and dignity. Who gave them that right? That someone would come down on a six-year-old with a stick. When I used to look at my grandchildren and think about that, that's what horrified me, the severity of the cruelty.

"I could deal with hunger but I can't deal with the emotional thing— you have no right to live. Once, I was told I was worse than the soldiers who crucified Christ. I was about six. They drummed into us how bad these people were; imagine then being told you were worse than them."

One day in 1963, exactly 10 years since she had arrived in Goldenbridge, Julie Cooney was told she had a visitor.

"I was 14. I remember one of the lay teachers told me to go to the villa, that's what we called it, where the visitors came. Before I opened the door of the villa, I could see her coming up. I recognised her when I saw her coming. It was a long time but I still recognised the face. It was my mother at the door.

"There were no hugs. I don't know what she said except 'you look after yourself.' There was no reason for hugs, I had no real feelings for her and I don't know why she decided to visit me that day. I've no idea. She's the only one who can answer that.

"She was married again by then and had four children. She never told her husband about us. The first time I saw her after I got married, her eldest son was married and had a child. I brought my daughter to see her and she said 'she's not half as nice as my grandchild.' What kind of a cold, calculating woman would say that. And, of course, she was her grandchild too. In all the years in the institutions, my mother never even sent us a birthday card or a Christmas card, or if she did, we didn't get it.

"The official court reason we were sent away was 'lack of parental guardianship'. But that doesn't wash with me. My mother had two stepchildren, aged about 20 and 17, and they would have been quite able to take care of us. The NSPCC (now ISPCC) has no records but they are supposed to have brought us in to the institutions. So who did? Did my mother call the NSPCC, I don't know. I do know she never told her husband about us. I was her first born. How could you do that? I went to see her when I came out. She was all about herself. I never went to see her again."

Julie Cooney's mother was killed while crossing the road in Swords, Co. Dublin, in 1979, at the age of 56. "When I went to her funeral," Julie says, "I wasn't recognized or acknowledged as her daughter."

Julie Cooney is a gentle, sophisticated, well-travelled woman. But her journeys have not been easy. She left Goldenbridge in 1965 at the age of 16 with very poor reading and writing skills and knew little about the purpose or function of money.

The nuns did find her a job and sent her to work as a cleaner to a doctor in Dublin but she was "treated like dirt. They'd give me my dinner on top of the washing machine" and she left after a fortnight. She then found a cleaning job at the Mater Hospital, where she stayed for 15 months. In 1967, she suffered from anorexia and was treated in hospital for that, and also for depression.

Other domestic jobs followed in Dublin but one job she found through an agency stands out for her. It was a child-minding job with a doctor in Ballsbridge. "She was my salvation, really. She was brilliant, absolutely brilliant," Julie Cooney recalls.

"When she finished at 4.30 or 5 I'd be finished too and I didn't have to work any weekends or anything. That was the first family I was ever connected to. She treated me so well. She included me in what the family were doing; she told me the facts of life; she brought me on holidays. She never took me for granted."

But then Julie found herself becoming too attached to the family. "I was getting a bit envious of what the children were getting and so on, of the good family they had. I was becoming too emotionally involved" and after working with the family for over a year she decided to leave. But she has kept in touch with the doctor over the years and remains very grateful to her.

Then, at the age of 21, in February 1970, Julie Cooney decided to go to America. "I just wanted to travel and I had a good friend there who'd been in care with me." Manhattan was her destination. She found a job in a pub on 34th Street. "I had a green card, so they thought I was the safest on the desk outside!"

She liked America but she knew she didn't want to live there forever. "It was strange. Ireland hadn't really offered me anything."

Nevertheless, in December 1972, she returned to Ireland. It would be a fateful decision because less than a year later, while on holiday in Wexford, she met the man who became her husband in April 1973.

Over the years, she and her husband had four children but they would also suffer the tragedy of the deaths of two of them soon after their birth. Julie also had to cope with the ever-present trauma of Goldenbridge and its impact on her children.

"There was very little emotion with my children. There was very little hugging. It wasn't intentional. The hardest thing to cope with is not being able to hug your own children."

It was not until her children had grandchildren that the pain and trauma began to abate. Julie Cooney clearly adores her three grandchildren with a love that is as complete as it is poignant. "I can hug my grandchildren but I couldn't hug my children. I could do material things for them but I couldn't do emotional things."

These emotional scars may endure for the rest of Julie Cooney's life. About 18 years ago when she happened to see a photograph of the nun who meted out punishment to the children on the landing at Goldenbridge terror seized her like a physical force. "I could not move," she said. "My whole insides drained."

"The lack of affection for any of us, that was the worst: the complete lack of humanity. Yet these were Christian people."

3

STORY OF DES MURRAY

*"Apart from the sheer terror, they obliterated human emotions.
I have an existence only, not a life. I'd love to have lived"*

There is a deep hole and trapped inside it is a young boy. He is covered in mud, struggling and terrified. He cries out but there is no one to help. Suddenly he is aware that light has begun to flood in. When he looks up, he can see broken glass at the mouth of the hole, shining brightly in the sun. He moves towards the light, leaving behind a vicious nightmare spawned at Artane Industrial School for Boys.

The light that flooded in was the two missing weeks of Des Murray's life, which he had blocked out for 40 years, after a savage attack by a Christian Brother. "I was over 50 when I got out of that bog hole," he says.

"I had always known there was a fortnight in Artane I couldn't account for, no explanation for it. It came back like a dam-burst 40 years later.

"I was sitting in a bus in Dublin in 1993 on my way to a counselling session. It all came flooding back. It was A, the voice inside my head said. It was Brother A who did it (name supplied).

"It was 1954. We were being marched at night to the dormitories. The door up to the dormitory had a light at it but there was a dark spot. The Brother was standing there and almost invisible to me. He stepped out of the dark. He just came at me. There was an explosion in my left ear. I must have blacked out. I thought I was dead.

"The next thing I can see this tiny gold circle, a lace (eyelet) and it's oscillating. It was the shoe and trousers and soutane, and the leg coming out of the soutane, and every time the leg came out I could feel my ribs break. I was almost unconscious. He was still kicking me. He hit me a blow nearly hard enough to knock me out. I couldn't escape him. I couldn't get out from under the weight. He was holding my ankles. He was holding me down like a vice grip. At that point, I wanted to die; he was going to kill me anyway.

"By deciding to die I had disassociated myself from it. I'd closed that time from my life. I vaguely remember three or four figures in green, medics probably; they must have drugged me after the attack. That's why I couldn't remember. That was my missing two weeks, maybe even longer than that. I didn't die in that sense but I certainly died psychologically, emotionally. It was like I had a lead helmet around my head; I was locked up inside myself and they threw away the key. It was nearly 40 years before I understood what had happened.

"Artane was a concentration camp," he says quietly. "I was singled out by two Brothers, two sadists. My biggest regret is that I didn't kill those two bastards.

"One was particularly savage. One fella I knew had a rheumatic heart but Brother B (name supplied) used to make him fill a wheelbarrow with stones and wheel it around the yard three or four times. Any time it suited him, he'd stop me in the yard and say, 'spell that' and he kept trying to get me. He knew I was clever. He hated that. Everyone swore I swallowed a dictionary. But he never got me."

Des had arrived in Artane at the age of 12½ in 1954, having already been moved through a number of institutions in Dublin.

He was the son of an unmarried mother and was born in 1941 in St Kevin's Hospital Dublin (now St. James's). A short time later, he was moved a few miles away to St Patrick's Mother and Baby Home on the Navan Road.

His first memory of the Mother and Baby home visibly terrifies him.

"I seem to have been in a small room, in a cot. The door opens and I see a big, tall man in black, but no features on the face. He comes in. He closes the door. I know I'm in the cot and I'm trying to get away from him. But my foot gets caught between the bars of the cot and I couldn't get away. I'm trying to get away from whoever this is. I'm in absolute terror."

"I have no proof, but I believe what was happening to me was an assault. I suspect the person was a priest, checking on the kids and that was what he was at."

He only has one memory of his mother at the Mother and Baby home. He is sitting on her lap and she's feeding him some cheese. "I remember it was nice cheese. That was the only memory I have of any interaction with her there."

From the Mother and Baby Home, he was moved a few years later to St Philomena's Convent in the south side of Dublin. That, too, would be traumatic.

"When I was five or six in the convent, this vicious nun boxed our ears if we came down late after making our beds. Then she took half your breakfast away. I started shouting at that, jumping up and down, and the chair broke under me. Then she took me to the head nun and told her and she pulled down my trousers and gave me 23 slaps on the bare backside."

Des's mother visited him often but he didn't tell her what it was like "because she'd blame me not the nuns, and they knew this."

"I never once in that place remember sitting out in the open, what you'd expect children to do. When we were in the building and in the yard we were watched all the time, it felt like a prison."

He recalls a "test" the nuns did to see how bright or otherwise the children were.

"They'd make a small balloon and they used to squeeze that on the foreheads of the kids. If it burst when they were pressing it, you were brainy. If it didn't burst you were as thick as 10 planks. It was nonsense, but this is what they did."

But he still remembers the kindness of one nun, Sr. Philomena, who rewarded him in class. "She asked the Irish word for gloves. She said she'd give sixpence to anyone who knew it. Nobody said it and I put up my hand and said, *'lamhini'*, and she gave me sixpence. It was the only time I ever remember being rewarded for anything."

Indeed, it is the only act of kindness that Des can recall in his 16 years in institutions. "I didn't know what kindness was. As an adult, I couldn't figure it out for a long time. It took me 10 years. I was very suspicious of anyone who was kind to me. To me, the possibility of decency or grace or integrity was non-existent."

In 1948, at the age of about 7½, Des was transferred from St Philomena's Convent to nearby Carriglea Park Industrial School for Senior Boys, run by the Christian Brothers, where he would spend the next five years of his life.

The Ryan Report tells us, perhaps somewhat ominously, that the Christian Brothers expected Carriglea to be an "Artane on a small scale." It was certified as an industrial school in 1894 and closed nearly 60 years later in 1954, around which time Des Murray was transferred to Artane.

Carriglea was a large institution, comparable with that at Letterfrack in Co Galway and bigger than those in Tralee in Co Kerry, Salthill in Co Galway or Glin in Co Limerick. The average number of pupils in the school ranged from a high of 260, in 1939 and 1945, to a low of 180 in 1952.

Throughout the 1940s, the numbers in Carriglea exceeded the certified limit of 250 boys, the Ryan Report said. Boys were admitted from the age of six and, between 1940 and 1954, part of the period during which Des Murray was there, 76 per cent of the children were between 9 and 12 years old.

Fear is Des Murray's dominant memory of the first day he arrived in Carriglea from St Philomena's – fear of the boys there, even more than the Brothers. His fears were well founded.

The Ryan Report says of Carriglea in the years before Des arrived:

> *"Documents show Carriglea to have been an unruly, chaotic and disorganised place from 1936 until 1945. Discipline was lacking, and sexual activity among the boys was widespread."*

"We left St Philomena's in this fancy car—it was big enough to carry seven of us in the back and there was a priest in the passenger seat. We arrived at a big gate and drove up an avenue." Once inside Carriglea, the boys were taken to a large room.

"It was probably a classroom. We were cowering in the room. We heard this cacophony of noise outside, shouting and everything; we were terrified. In the convent, we couldn't say boo, we didn't understand what all this noise was. I got brave, or reckless, and I stood up on a chair and looked out and saw this concourse, with what looked like thousands of fellas a lot older than me; it looked like mayhem.

"They let us out into the yard later on. We were terrified; we were convinced we were going to be killed. I'd never seen a hurley till then; I didn't know what they were. Later on I asked my mother when she came one Sunday – she'd come up nearly every Sunday – if she'd get me one. Of course, I realized if I had one I could use it to defend myself against the bigger fellas and the bullying. I'd let them have it if they came near me. I learned pretty quickly how to use a hurley."

Des Murray learned how to do most things pretty quickly. He got a good primary education in Carriglea, where the Brothers found out he was clever. About a decade ago, an educational psychologist determined that Des has an IQ of 147, which is regarded as "very superior intelligence" and is a score better than 99.9 per cent of the general population. But in the perverse environment of Carriglea, being a bright young boy was simply an additional burden.

"First and second class were in the same room, and if the Brother was too busy with second class he'd ask me to come up and teach first. I ended up being ostracised and I suffered a lot of bullying, because they saw everybody as 'them and us'. And when I was doing that, I was one of 'them'. So for that reason it was as well I was able to defend myself. I suppose I was ostracised all the time after that."

But it was in Carriglea too that Des learned about music: something which he still credits with helping "to retain my sanity." He learned to play the flute and the coronet and was naturally talented. It came at a price, but his talent for music would prove invaluable years later in Artane.

"In the band at Carriglea, we had a brutal man. He had a black ebony drumstick: it was a heavy one and if he didn't like what you were doing, he'd throw it at you. Every instrument in Carriglea had dents on it from us protecting ourselves. There didn't have to be a reason, the man was mad. He never hit you where it could be seen. He was cute; he'd been in the guards."

In 1954, the year that Carriglea closed, Des was transferred to Artane at the age of 12½. But none of the boys were told where they were going. "I was in charge of organising the laundry and I wondered why there were no clothes out for the next day. Word began to spread but no one told us anything and we only knew we were leaving when we saw three buses that morning. They knew we were aware of Artane's reputation, so they didn't want to tell us."

In Artane, Des's character would profoundly change.

"Artane changed me. I wasn't an offensive kid. That changed immediately I went to Artane. I went in as a timid young fella. In 12 to18 months, I could kill. Sometimes I wish I had."

But brutal as it was for Des in Artane, he undoubtedly escaped some of the physical and sexual savagery there by joining the Artane Boys Band.

He joined the band very quickly after arriving in Artane. "Brother Joseph knew he didn't have to teach us because we'd been in the band at Carriglea. I played the trumpet and when they had too many trumpets players, I played the trombone and later, the drums.

"Brother Joseph was in charge and he instilled in us that we had to leave disputes outside and behave in the band and he said if we didn't behave he'd come down on us like a ton of bricks. The other Brothers were also afraid of Brother Joseph so they left us alone. Also, in the band we'd go out often to Croke Park, so the Brothers were afraid we might talk, or if we were beaten too much, people would see that too, so in that sense I escaped them."

Soon, Des rose to become leader of the band. It happened partly by accident. "Someone else was picked before me but he couldn't bring the band to a halt properly, imagine if you couldn't do that in Croke Park, so they picked me then. I was thinking of the responsibility more than anything else. You had to have presence, they said. I didn't know what it was, but they said I had that and of course they knew I could play all the instruments."

Des Murray witnessed sexual violence in Artane but did not encounter it directly himself. "I remember seeing a Brother on the landing and he was spotting the boys. They carefully chose their victims. You wouldn't see the boys going into the Brothers' room, but sometimes you'd see them running out, screaming. They chose the vulnerable ones. I suppose it also helped that my mother visited regularly.

"I also had a gang of Carriglea boys and we'd try to protect each other from the Artane boys and the Brothers. Our hurleys had been sent on from Carriglea, so we knew we could defend ourselves. Whenever they took them off us, we'd find them and hide them. I used to put them in the priest's section of the confessional box and then move them around to other places.

"When we went to Artane the Carriglea boys stuck together. We'd come from the same system but it was different. Artane was absolutely vicious but they believed it was good, we didn't. In Carriglea, there were rules. You got two slaps or four slaps or six slaps, no more, and the Brothers kept the rules. But in Artane, there were no rules; they hit you as much as they wanted and they encouraged the Artane boys to bully us. We had to protect each other, Buffalo and I and about 10 others in the Carriglea gang. They tried to put manners on us."

Des is measured in the words he chooses, but twice in interviews, he uses the term 'concentration camp' to describe Artane. Yet the term hardly seems out of place as he describes how the Brothers 'tried to put manners' on them.

The Brothers spoke to the Artane boys and quietly arranged a battle between them and the unsuspecting Carriglea boys. Then, from behind windows, as the terrifying fight ensued in the yard outside, the Brothers gathered to watch.

"No one had ever beaten Artane in the shop leagues, so they played us, they went at us. We had no warning. Pure concentration camp, the Brothers arranged the battle and watched.

"There were 800 boys in that yard, 100 Carriglea boys and about 700 Artane fellas at the other end. I was out in the yard with a hurley and ball. There was this dead silence. The Artane boys at the other end looked like they were congregating for something. Then I noticed Brothers filing into the main building. They were gathering to watch from the windows. I thought there was something serious going on. The Brothers were deliberately fomenting the Artane boys. We knew something was up. I told Buffalo. I gathered all the Carriglea fellas. I told Buffalo where I'd hidden the hurleys and they ran off for them."

As he eyed the Artane boys, Des suddenly remembered his favourite story from an English book at Carriglea. It was about the Battle of Thermopylae in 480 BC when fewer than 4,000 Spartan and other Greek soldiers held off an army of several hundred thousand Persians for three days, giving the rest of Greece time to regroup.

The Greeks were able to hold off the Persians because of how and where they fought. The mountain pass was so narrow that the Greeks only had to face a small number of the Persians at a time. The Greeks had 10 rows and 10 columns of soldiers carrying twelve-foot long spears and because of the tight formation and shields, practically no part of a soldier was unprotected. "I always liked the story, it was inspiring," Des recalls.

Two and a half thousand years later, in Des's mind, the Artane boys numbering 700 were the Persians and the 100 Carriglea boys were the

Greeks. But crucially, like the Greeks, the Carriglea boys were also armed with lethal weapons – hurleys.

"There were 700 of them, about 100 of us. I said 'we're dead, they'd been told to get us.' We only had one chance.

"We made three lines in a curly } bracketed formation, with Buffalo and myself leading and the others around the sides. The guys with no weapons were at the back. Slowly you could hear a bzzzzzzzz, like a hornet's nest, the sinister sound of the Artane fellas. We charged from the two walls in the yard and then stopped.

"The Artane fellas thought we were finished. Then, as the hornets' nest crescendo built up, they came towards us and we charged again. They were taken by surprise. We circled them before they knew what was happening and attacked them from a position of ambush. We flattened them. We could see the wall of bodies melting away. We didn't realise how tough we were.

"It was a real battlefield. I think some of them were taken to the infirmary and a few Carriglea boys too."

One "inhuman" act of cruelty that he witnessed still stands out for him over half a century later.

"I saw it happening twice to this poor fella. There were about 200 of us with Brother C (name supplied) and we were walking on the road, now Kylemore Road, and there was a pile of stones and gravel left by road works. One day Brother C told this boy to kneel on the gravel. Then he started picking up some of the small stones and started flicking them at him. He was stoning the kid on the gravel.

"One day a stranger, or maybe he was a local man, saw what was happening and he came over and told the Brother if he caught him doing that again he'd kill him. We were amazed at this man, taking on the power of Artane. I thought you couldn't challenge the religious. I couldn't understand a man confronting authority. But after that I never saw the Brother doing it again."

Des Murray was discharged from Artane at the age of 16, in 1957.

"I just wanted to get out. You knew on your birthday you'd be out. You got a suit the night before and brought anything you had in a case. I wanted to bring nothing. Just to get out. I remember no one said goodbye. I walked out the avenue and on the way, I saw one of the sadists. I was sorry later I didn't kill that Brother."

That winter morning in 1957, Des got a bus from Artane to the city centre and from there across to Glasthule on the south side, where his mother worked and where her employers had found her a cottage.

Des felt a great sense of freedom as he made his way to Glasthule, the bus passing a few fliers on lampposts from the election a few months earlier that had brought 75-year-old Eamon de Valera and his Fianna Fáil party to power. But such events meant little to Des Murray. "I remembered hearing the name as 'Yamon' de Valera once in Artane, and I thought it was a very strange name. That was all I knew about politics"

After about six months in Glasthule, Des moved with his mother, in 1958, to Fitzwilliam St, where she had got a housekeeping job. He would live in that house for most of the next 46 years, moving only about a decade ago to a Dublin Corporation flat. His mother died in 1994 at the age of 84. His mother had visited him regularly in Artane but, nevertheless, their relationship was fraught.

Des says his mother blamed him for her predicament. She didn't talk to him and he says he couldn't talk to her. "She lived to be 84 and she never, ever told me a single word about who my father was. I only found out when I was 20 that I had cousins when my mother's sister visited from England. I didn't know who she was till then and she had eight kids in England. That's when I found out I had an aunt and cousins."

Des found it difficult to adapt to life outside the institutions. For a long time, the most ordinary things were extraordinary challenges for him. "I found things like using money, ordinary things like having a conversation very difficult. I didn't know what to talk about or how to talk to anyone, so no one would talk to me. I didn't know what a conversation was. I couldn't talk about politics, or sex or religion or whatever, I just didn't know how. I thought I was mad."

In the mid-Sixties Des studied at UCD for about a year and in 1967 he went to London. But he didn't like the city and after a few months, he returned to Dublin, where he eventually opened a tailoring business. After he fell ill, the business declined in the Eighties and after it closed, he became a contract tailor.

About 13 years ago, Des saw Buffalo coming out of the GPO in Dublin. They had lost touch since Artane but they recognised one another instantly. Then, almost as quickly, they each continued walking their separate ways on O'Connell Street. "I think neither of us wanted to disturb the memories, like disturbing coals, we didn't want to stoke the fire into rage."

Des's adult years have been mostly suffused with pain, filled with horrors and nightmares that he could never hide from. "It was a life sentence but we didn't commit a crime. We weren't flesh and blood to them; we were numbers, nothing, a sin to be punished. We were like dust or mould to blow away.

"It was only later you realised they took all your spirit away from you, they took everything. They knew all of this fear. It was calculated. It wasn't accidental. They subsumed you into a kind of android state.

"Apart from the sheer terror, they obliterated human emotions. That's why I call Artane a concentration camp—it was a complete de-humanising process.

"They knew exactly what they were doing. It was a plan and they followed it unswervingly, unquestioningly, intuitively. They were like complete automatons. They were conveyor-belted into these institutions. If you were a second or third daughter and you weren't going to get married, you were a nun. It was the same with the second and third sons: they joined the Christian Brothers.

"And they were doing the same with the children in the courts, like conveyor belts, sending them off to the institutions.

"I have sympathy for the decent nuns or Brothers but they were all made part of this. These Brothers and nuns committed emotional murder and suicide. It caused deadness in you and as you grew older it was the horror of that that hit you."

For Des Murray it was the horror of losing love because the deadness within him left him unable to recognise it, to express it or to accept it.

It took him 25 years to recognise the love he felt for two men. And, by then, it was too late. "I didn't know until they died that I loved them. I wasn't able to express it and I had no ability to do anything about it. I'd been deadened inside, unable to love, to be fulfilled spiritually and physically. It took me 25 years to see this." And when he finally saw it, he put the love he lost into verse:

The Hawthorn Tree

They buried "1" near the hawthorn tree in a Sunday suit of clothes,
They buried "1" near the hawthorn tree the body to dispose.
They buried "1" near the hawthorn tree; they didn't ask "1", they wouldn't ask me,
If we were ready yet to decompose.

They buried "2" near the hawthorn tree in a fine spring morning rain,
They buried "2" near the hawthorn tree in a pall of numbing pain.
They buried "2" near the hawthorn tree; they didn't ask "two". no need to ask me,
If we would wish to pass this way again.

They'll bury "3" near the hawthorn tree, no pall, no pain, no clothes,
They'll bury me near the hawthorn tree in case I get up their nose.
They'll bury me near the hawthorn tree, no-one left to ask, too late to ask me
If they should seek our pardon in repose.

More recently, he put another kind of love into poetry:

Helen

Thou mindst me of a summer's day,
When sun o'erlights the fields of May,
And sends the hedgerows on their way,
In joyous exultation.

And of the moon so shining bright,
Whose wondrous, pale candescent light,
Turns all the seas and oceans white,
In jealous imitation.

But neither sun nor moon e'er say,
Why went they on their endless way,
But I suspect, if asked, they'd say
"In Helen's admiration."

Des Murray, now almost 73, finds some release from his horrors in classical music also. "It helps me to retain my sanity," he says. "It always has. I have endured, that's what I've done with my life. But endurance is just an existence, like a stone statue in the rain. I have an existence only, not a life.

"I'd love to have lived."

4

STORY OF VALENTINE WALSH

"I was sexually abused between the ages of 9 and 13"

Valentine Walsh shows a photograph of himself as a little boy. He is seven years old and it is the day of his First Holy Communion.

He looks very handsome, this little boy, with his dark hair and his spiffy suit and tie, but Valentine isn't smiling.

He doesn't ever remember a reason to smile. All Valentine Walsh remembers is the terror.

A locked door, a darkened room and three Christian Brothers who sexually and physically abused him.

That is the world that lay in wait for the little boy in the Communion group of 1960, in St Joseph's Industrial School, Tralee, Co. Kerry.

Valentine Walsh was born on February 21, 1953, at St Kevin's Hospital, Dublin, to an unmarried mother, Mary Walsh.

Within six days, mother and son would be separated from each other for most of the next 16 years of Valentine's life.

"On the second of March 1953, my mother was transferred to St John of Gods. She mustn't have been able to look after me. This must be why I was sent to the different places."

Valentine himself was also transferred from St Kevin's and taken a few miles away, to St Patrick's mother and baby home on the Navan Road, where he remained until he was three years old.

As Christmas approached in 1956, Valentine was sent south of the city, to St Philomena's in Stillorgan. Then, three days after his fourth birthday, on February 24, 1957, he was sent back to St Kevin's Hospital for six months because of an illness, and then he was taken back again to St Philomena's.

It was a dizzying number of moves for a little boy not yet five and Valentine has no memory of any of them. But he would be forever haunted by the fifth and final move.

On August 18, 1959, Valentine was transferred to St Joseph's Industrial School in Tralee, Co Kerry.

He was now just six-and-a-half and here, over the next decade, he would have his childhood wrenched from him and in its place would be left a lifetime of darkness and horror.

Valentine Walsh is visibly pained and angry when he speaks, but he recalls the shocking details in a firm, matter-of-fact voice.

"I was sexually abused between the ages of 9 and 13.

"I was abused by a number of Brothers during the 10 years I was there." (He names two Brothers who sexually abused him and names one Brother who physically abused him.)

"My first teacher there was Brother D (name supplied). After that I was taught by Brother E (name supplied) and finally by Brother F (name supplied).

"The first memory I have of being sexually abused by Brother D was when I was 9 or 10.

"He would take me into his own classroom in the evening when it was empty. He would lock the door behind us."

He recalls how it happened and how Brother D prepared the room for this hell.

"I remember the blackboard in the classroom was used by Brother D to block off the windows.

"Other clippings and newspaper were on the windows and blocked off any sight into the classroom. The clippings and the blackboard prevented anyone from the outside looking in. We were locked in and they were locked out."

Then the terror began.

"He would pull my trousers down around my knees and start pulling at my penis. He would pull up his robe and take out his penis, and get me to pull at his penis. I didn't know what was involved at the time but he was forcing me to masturbate him and he also masturbated me. I believe it lasted about 20 minutes.

"It happened a number of times, as many as five or six times. I didn't understand initially what was happening and thought this was normal. But I didn't talk to my friends about it as it embarrassed me."

The abuse by Brother D went on for about two years.

"I remember Brother D as the teacher who taught me for that period and when I moved to a different class at the age of 11 or 12, the abuse stopped."

But only by Brother D.

Another predator lay in wait and, from the ages of about 11 to 13, Valentine Walsh was sexually abused by Brother E.

One of the places this happened was in the children's dormitory. By some merciful act of God, Brother E waited until the children's room was empty before sexually assaulting Valentine Walsh.

"Brother E sexually abused me in the children's dormitory on maybe four occasions. The abuse would happen during the day when the other children weren't in the room.

"The abuse would happen while I was lying on a bed and E would pull down my trousers. I remember him playing with his penis in front of me and forcing me to touch his penis."

As well as being sexually assaulted, Valentine Walsh also suffered violent physical abuse during the same period.

This started at the age of about 9 or 10 and lasted until he left the primary school to go to a local secondary school at about 13 years of age.

"I remember Brother F. It was for being bold. It was in the recreation room. He would put my head between his knees, pull down my pants, and beat me with the strap on the bare backside.

"He would beat me nine or ten times on the backside, sometimes it could be more, sometimes less."

As well as the unrelenting emotional suffering, Valentine Walsh still carries a physical reminder of this Brother's brutality.

"Once I tried to run away from him and he struck me on the right leg with his strap. I have a scar to this day from the blow from the strap."

The abuse stopped when he left primary school. Valentine continued to live at the Christian Brothers institution while attending a local secondary school.

"I left the Christian Brothers when I was 16 years of age and I remember my mother collecting me and bringing me to Dublin."

In the intervening years, he had seen little of his mother who had subsequently married. Valentine lived with them for a short while, but then the marriage broke up and soon after that, Valentine left home and began living rough on the streets of Dublin.

"I felt I had received a poor education and felt ill-trained for anything. I spent a lot of time in the workshops, making footballs for Gaelic players, and sewing socks."

Life on the streets was harsh. Soon he got in with a gang and started a life of pretty crime.

"My job was robbing pushbikes, handbags, clothes. I assaulted policemen. I drank heavily."

Just one year after leaving the hell that had been St Joseph's, Valentine found himself incarcerated again and he would spend most of the next 20 years of his life in and out of prison.

"I went to prison first when I was 17 years of age for robbing a pushbike. I was sent to Marlborough House."

About a year later, at the age of 18, he was sentenced to prison again. This time he got six months for assaulting a garda.

His criminal activity intensified. Soon he was convicted for selling drugs and got five years in Mountjoy Prison. "I was regularly involved in fights and on one occasion my nose was broken."

Valentine would make an attempt to break the cycle of crime and punishment, but from the start, he would be doomed to fail.

In 1974, he joined the Irish Army, having lied about his criminal record.

After just six months, he was court marshalled for being absent without leave and was dishonourably discharged.

It was a time of turbulence, but it also became a time of hope and then of love.

"At 22 years of age I married. In between periods of my incarceration, I lived with her for 13 years." They had two children, a boy and a girl, who are now grown up.

But the violence that had consumed Valentine Walsh's life would now destroy his marriage.

"The relationship I had with my wife was quite violent. I was barred from the house. I feel a lot of guilt about this. I had a serious alcohol problem."

But before they separated, Valentine Walsh told his wife about the sexual and physical abuse he suffered in St Joseph's. Over the years, he told his children too.

"It took me 33 years before I could speak about the abuse. It took me a long time but I ended up telling my wife. I had to tell her. It was doing my head in. Then my marriage broke up, my wife left me.

"I've had a serious alcohol problem for a number of years. Counselling has helped me and I no longer drink from morning time. I still take a drink, but I feel more in control of it."

Valentine Walsh had his last extended period in prison in 1988. "I lived in boarded up houses, squatting." At other times, he lived on the streets.

Petty crime and drink had become a way of life. "I was living rough. This day it was really bad, I was very drunk and some young fellas started pouring paint on me. I got away into the pub. Soon after that I met this fella in the pub and I was telling him about the abuse and he said he'd bring me to a place."

That place, as it turned out, would be Valentine's salvation. It was the Aislinn Education and Support Centre for Survivors of Institutional Abuse, which was then based on Dublin's Ormond Quay.

"I was afraid to go in, I was drunk, but I kept coming back. Then I stopped drinking and came back and when I stopped drinking, I was able to do things. I've been coming to the centre for over 13 years now. Only for this place I'd have stayed drinking or I'd be locked up," he says, recalling how Aislinn co-founder the late Christine Buckley personally negotiated his release from Mountjoy over a decade ago.

"Christine went to Mountjoy once for me. She wrote a letter and talked to the judge and got me out. I was selling lighters with no licence and got a month.

"Christine came up to Lonergan (then prison governor John Lonergan) and told him all about the abuse I went through. Lonergan said 'get your belongings you're going back to Aislinn.' Christine drove me to the centre. I never went back to prison since."

It is worth noting that when Mr Lonergan retired in 2010 he said he hoped he would be remembered for taking a genuine interest in prisoners and for having a fair and just regime. Certainly, that is how he will be remembered by Valentine Walsh.

Eventually, Valentine got accommodation from Dublin Corporation.

He has also since forged a good relationship with his wife and family, with the help of the Aislinn centre. He now sees his wife frequently and when she suffered an illness in the summer of 2011, Valentine saw her every day and cooked for her.

He also credits his son, now in his 30s, for helping the relationship "I was at a bar and someone pointed out my son. I hadn't seen him for a few years. My son said he'd take me home. My wife opened the door and left me in and we started talking. I see her nearly every day now. My son and my wife help me now and I help them. I'm closer to my son than my daughter." Valentine's son is now working in Spain and comes home regularly to see his parents.

Valentine has begun to notch up other achievements, too, at the Aislinn centre. He is known to serve up a great Mexican stew at the cookery classes.

He has 14 Fetac (Further Education and Training Awards Council) certificates and is particularly proud of the fact that he now has a Level 6 Advanced Certificate in multimedia communications – Level 3 is the equivalent of Junior Certificate level and 4/5 is the equivalent of Leaving Certificate level. He even jokes sometimes about how smart he is and when he smiles for an instant, his face is no longer in pain.

But that is an illusion.

The torment never leaves Valentine Walsh. It haunts him every day and every night.

"I have nightmares all the time. I'm a loner. I live by myself. I only feel safe on my own. I can't trust people. I couldn't trust the Brothers, from an early age. They were bastards. After that, forget about anyone. I don't want to know anyone.

"I believe I have felt sad for as long back as I can remember. Most of my life between the years of 1969 and 1988 has been spent in corrective institution as a result of my behaviour."

Valentine went to Tralee once in the late 1970s. He wasn't sure why he went down or what he was looking for. Perhaps he had an idea of confronting his tormentors.

But Valentine found that the Brothers were visiting Dublin and he describes how he finally tracked them down in Henry Street.

"I followed them. They went into Woolworths. I ran after them. They must have seen me and they escaped. They went down the Ilac centre and then they must have disappeared. I've never seen them since. I would have killed them. But it would have been worse for me if I had. I'm glad I didn't.

"What's done can't be undone. I can't forgive or forget that. I can never forgive. I can never forget what happened to me."

A former brother at St Joseph's described the institution to the Ryan investigation as "A secret, enclosed world, run on fear".

Valentine Walsh remembers that fear. "It was there all the time even if they weren't abusing you. There was nobody there. They did what they liked.

"You were inferior life. You were whipped or whatever they wanted to do with you.

"I couldn't run away. I had nowhere to run. I was only a young fella. That was how it was."

One of the most chilling aspects of Valentine Walsh's story is his despair that even now, over half a century later, no one has faced justice for the crimes perpetrated against that "young fella".

"They should go to jail. Money has nothing to do with it. They should be jailed for what they did. You know, I know that they'll get away with it.

"I went to jail for what I did. If that was me, I'd go to jail. They'll get away with it.

"They'll never be jailed."

5

STORY OF PAT LAMBERT

Abuse in confessional, sacristy, dormitory

Four boys have just brought cows to fresh pasture. The boys are tired and the lush green grass seems the perfect place to rest for a while on a bright summer's day. The daisies catch their eye.

One of the boys starts to make a daisy chain, picking them at just the right length, carefully making a slit in the stem with his nail, adding one, then another, as the chain gets longer and longer until he ties it end to end. Then he places the chain of flowers around Pat Lambert's neck.

"I had four of them around my neck," Pat recalls, over 70 years later. "Twister Ryan had this way of making them. I can still see him and the other two boys in the field with the daisies around us."

It may be a testament to Bert Lambert's resilience that he still holds such an idyllic scene among his tormented memories of Artane Industrial School for Boys in Dublin. Or, maybe it was the terror of what happened next that seared that day into his mind forever.

"We'd taken the cows out to the field. On our way back, we were tired so we sat down to have a rest. I remember the sun was shining. We started to pick the daisies and lost all sense of time. The Brother in charge of the dairy came looking for us. He said we were trying to run away and brought us in front of Brother G (name supplied).

"He gave us a right leathering with the strap, on our hands, legs, everywhere. Then he took us to the (school) barber. He told him to shave our heads. Then he put us on display at a school window, with a placard around our necks saying, 'This is what happens to anyone who tries to run away.'

"All the boys were called into the yard and Brother G told them all privileges (like, for example, being allowed home on a Sunday or taken out to a match or a weekend break once in a while) were stopped. All of this was because of us and Brother G told the boys they could do what they liked to us. Consequently, we were kicked, punched and spat at.

"This punishment went on for six weeks. It happened at 11 School – that was where all the punishment was meted out. Even when we went to the toilet, we had to have two older boys or a Brother as monitors. The door of the toilet was left open in case we tried to escape."

It was into this hellish environment that 10-year-old Pat Lambert was delivered for six years on foot of a sentence by a court of the Irish State on November 12, 1942, after he was wrongly accused, yet nevertheless convicted, of stealing £1 from the County Home in Enniscorthy, Co. Wexford.

Pat had lived in the County Home with his mother, brother and three sisters while his father sought work as a casual labourer. When their father found work, usually in the summer, the family would move from the Home to live with him.

Pat was eight when he saw his father for the last time.

"I remember him coming along the road and hearing him shouting about joining the (British) army to fight the Germans because they'd dropped a bomb in Wexford."

The wartime bombings that had so unnerved Pat Lambert's father occurred on August 26, 1940, when the German Air Force dropped five bombs on the county. One hit the Shelburne Co-operative Creamery in Campile, not far from Foulkesmill, where the Lamberts were living that summer.

"We were out in the road. We saw a huge plane and two smaller ones. We watched and watched. Then we heard a thud. Then, another thud. There were three or four thuds in all. Three people were killed and my father was shouting 'I'm going to fight the Germans'. The next thing he was gone. I never saw my dad again."

Pat, his mother, brother and sisters returned to the County Home in Enniscorthy. Pat didn't mind the Home too much. The nuns regarded him as a trustworthy boy. At the age of nine, he was given a major responsibility – to look after the contents of an important room.

In that room were eight half-crowns and eight pieces of plug tobacco. His job was to distribute them to eight elderly men in the Home each Saturday about one o'clock.

"Sister Rumold trusted me to give the men a big lump of plug tobacco – I think it was Clarks – and a half crown. I'd get the key, open the door and give the men their quota."

But one Saturday, Pat made a decision that would plunge the next six years of his life into a brutal abyss.

"One Saturday Tom, one of the other boys, said to me 'why don't you leave that window open'. It never dawned on me; never dawned on me to even ask why. I wasn't well up, and I left it ajar. Imagine, I was that foolish. Next time when I went in, there was only the tobacco. There were no half crowns in sight. The men wanted to know what happened to the money. There was pandemonium. They must have gone to Sister Rumold.

"On Sunday morning, Tom and his two brothers and myself were in the town, and we were passing a shop and Tom gave me a half-crown and asked me to get sweets in the shop; so I went in. He didn't." Pat laughs at the foolishness of it now. "A half a crown then was a week's wages. The lady in the shop must have called the guards. They arrived and took us all to the station.

"I found out later in the court document (which he showed me) I was accused of 'feloniously relieving Sister Rumold of the sum of £1 or eight half crowns.'

"We went down to the court in Enniscorthy. My mammy was there as well. Tom and his brothers, Michael and James, had no-one with them. When the sentence was given out that we were to be detained until 16 years of age, my mammy screamed her head off. The policemen had to take her out of the court, still screaming."

Soon Pat and the three brothers would begin their journey to Artane in Dublin. But first, the garda showed Pat an act of kindness that he still remembers with gratitude.

"Out of the kindness of his heart, the policeman took me back to the County Home to say goodbye to my mother after sentence was passed."

Their goodbye took place on the steps of the Home on a cold winter morning, a month before Christmas 1942.

"I wasn't crying, but she was, the poor woman. I walked up the steps, the policeman behind me. Two nuns were beside her at the top of the steps. There was a hug and a kiss. She gave me 6d and said 'here, get something for yourself when you can.' Then I was gone. I never had a chance to say goodbye to my brother or sisters. The policeman took me and the three brothers to the train in Enniscorthy, and said we were going on a nice, long train journey.

"I found out later that soon after we were taken away my mother was put in the mental hospital. She suffered a lot. She was there for two years. I didn't see her again for almost 10 years."

However, Pat would spend almost all of those years believing his mother and all his family were dead because that's what he was told soon after he arrived in Artane.

"It was my first day in class. Brother H (name supplied) called me up to the blackboard to spell my name in Irish. When I couldn't he hit me across the back of the head and called me all the names under the sun. He shouted I was an imbecile, an amadan and made me repeat the names after him. 'Is it any wonder all belonging to you are dead,' he said. I thought for years they were all dead because of my stupidity."

In the Ireland of the Forties, and indeed over the next five decades, it is quite likely that few would have believed the horrors that made up daily life in Artane. "Thank God we're believed now. I'm delighted I lived to see the Ryan Report (in 2009) which vindicated us." Yet as far back in 1948, when Pat Lambert was being released from Artane, official Ireland was well aware of conditions in Artane and other institutions.

The Ryan investigation of institutional child abuse noted in its landmark report that in 1946, for example, a former resident of Artane complained to the Department of Education about conditions in the institution.

Initially, his complaints related to the primitive sanitation system in operation in the institution. Then, in a letter dated 6th November, this former resident stated:

> *"It is 11 yrs since I was in Artane and I don't forget one minute of it; neither do others. The injustices done to others and myself, I will see (it) won't happen to others: Boys beaten, under the Shower Baths ... Boys heads beaten on the Handball Alley Wall ... and a Drill Master who used say, 'do it where you stand' when a boy asked to go to the W.C."*

But in a memorandum dated 8th November 1946, cited by the Ryan Report, the Assistant Secretary in the Department of Education agreed with the Inspector that no action was required in response to this letter. No response was sent to the former resident and no comment was sought from the Resident Manager in Artane.

State and Church authorities also brushed aside scathing comments the same year by the Irish-American priest Fr Edward Flanagan, founder of the famous Boys Town USA, who visited Artane and St Patrick's in Belfast.

He was dismayed at the state of Ireland's reform schools and described them as "a scandal, un-Christ like, and wrong." It emerged in 2004 from Boys' Town archivist Tom Lynch that Fr Flanagan had gone even further after his 1946 visit. Mr Lynch told the late Mary Raftery that Fr Flanagan had talked about the Irish institutions being like "concentration camps for children."

As Fergus O'Dowd TD, noted in the Dáil debate on the Ryan Report on June 11, 2009, "Fr Flanagan's words fell on stony ground. He was simply ignored. The then Minister for Justice Gerald Boland said in the Dáil that he was 'not disposed to take any notice of what Monsignor Flanagan said while he was in this country, because his statements were so exaggerated that I did not think people would attach any importance to them.'"

Deputy O'Dowd, now Minister of State, added: "There were plenty of voices then and plenty of strong voices at the top of the Department of Education and from those involved in child care in other countries who commented on what happened. Yet we allowed it to happen, and it continued to happen."

In another infamous case in 1946, Limerick Councillor Martin McGuire and others in the city were shocked when 14-year-old Gerard Fogarty was flogged naked with a cat of nine tails and immersed in salt water for trying to escape to his mother from Glin Industrial School. Yet a call for a public inquiry into industrial schools was rejected by the Minister of Education, Thomas Derrig, because "it would serve no useful purpose".

Such an impenetrable wall of silence would facilitate the criminal abuse of children for another five decades. Clearly there would be no-one to look out for 10-year-old Pat Lambert in Artane during the six years he was detained there, from the winter of 1942 until the spring of 1948.

When Pat arrived in Artane there were 810 boys detained there. It was clear to him from the very first day that brutality was the only way of life.

"I went to Artane on the 11th November 1942 with the three brothers from Waterford. We went to Dublin by train and then walked all the way to Artane. When we got to Artane, we were examined by two Christian Brothers.

"Before we got examined I heard one of the Brothers say to strip to one of the Waterford boys. The oldest boy must have questioned the order. The next thing the Brother knocked him to the ground and said 'you're here now to do what you're told.'

"While I was getting examined, my eyes, my ears, throat, everywhere, I had to spread my arms out wide. I had the tanner (6d) my mother gave me when I left the County Home in my hand and it fell on the floor. I bent down to pick it up and got a clout across the back of my head from the Brother. He shouted 'you only do things here when you're told to'. Then we were told to pick up our clothes and to follow the Brother across the yard, naked, for haircuts and showers.

"We were showered with what must have been Jeyes fluid, because it scalded our eyes and privates. We all stepped back out of the showers in shock. The Brother shouted to us to get back in again and beat us across the backs, backsides and legs. I got seven lashes with the strap and the three others got the same. The showers were freezing cold and the pain from the beating was unbearable when we went back under the shower.

"We all got a number. It was stamped on our clothes. Mine was 11713. They'd use your number more than your name. In the classroom, the Brother would say 'stand up 11713'.

"I'd get hit in the classroom if I couldn't spell a word or read something. I'd be hit with a strap, a pointer, boxed in the head and face and hit on the backside with a hurley, whatever they had."

Pat got little schooling, usually just two and a half hours in the evening after a day working in the kitchens or farm.

The boys who attended school in the evening, the Ryan investigation said, "Did so after a long day working in a trade or on the farm. They were exhausted by the time they got to school, and did not even have time to change out of their work clothes before class."

Pat describes it thus: "When I was 12, I was put to work in the kitchen, farm and dairy farm. It was great in the kitchen and dairy farm because you got lots to eat. We used to eat the raw turnips and oats that the cows got. We'd take a pint of milk and replace it with water in the churn.

"One Saturday morning when I was in the dairy I saw a boy run over by a pigswill lorry. Charlie McGregor was his name. I was on the outside and Charlie was on the inside, one of the huge barrels on the lorry came down on him and he went right under the wheel of the lorry, crushed. It was an awful thing to see." Pat shudders, breathes deeply and continues: "The Brothers shouted at us to move on. I often wonder if Charlie had parents and were they told about it."

In 1944, two years after Pat Lambert arrived in Artane, the school band was getting ready to entertain thousands of fans in nearby Croke Park at the All-Ireland football final between Roscommon and Kerry. Kerry was the uncrowned king of Gaelic football by 1944, having already won 15 All-Ireland titles, and was favoured to capture the Sam Maguire Cup again that Sunday.

But in a dramatic game in front of 79,294 fans, the largest attendance at a sporting event ever held in Ireland up to then, Roscommon defeated the favourites by two points; the final score was Roscommon 1-09 Kerry 2-04. Among the record attendance was Pat Lambert.

"Brother I (name supplied) had a cousin or some relative playing on the Kerry team and brought 40 of us from 9 School to the match." Pat recalls that day, September 24, 1944, and what happened subsequently as a recurring nightmare.

"The match wasn't quite over when Brother I left. He was mad over Kerry losing. He made us run all the way back to the school. On Monday, we got the mother and father of a hiding from him because Kerry got beaten. He had us for Irish. He was still mad because of the match. He asked us something, myself, another boy Donal and a boy to our left. We didn't know the answer. The boy to our left was hit on the face with a duster that burst his eye. I got 100 slaps and a punch in the back of the head. I went flying head first into a cast iron radiator. I split my lower lip badly and my wrists were so swollen from the beating that I couldn't take my gansy off for three nights."

Pat Lambert's voice cracks. He pauses. He finds the courage to continue: "Donal was brought up to the front and put across the desk and got the strap across the bare backside. He carried on hitting and hitting him and punched him in the face. Donal fell on the floor and Brother I walked on his head." Pat shudders. He pauses again. "I heard 10 years ago that Donal McGrath died that night. That he committed suicide."

Pervasive, uncontrolled violence such as that encountered by Pat Lambert would be described 60 years later in the Ryan Report, thus:

> *"Artane used frequent and severe punishment to impose and enforce a regime of militaristic discipline. The policy of the School was rigid control by means of severe corporal punishment and fear of punishment. Such punishment was excessive and pervasive. The result of arbitrary and uncontrolled punishment was a climate of fear."*

But even more harrowing for Pat Lambert was the rampant sexual abuse that he witnessed or encountered directly himself.

Two years after he arrived and one month short of his 12th birthday, Pat was abused in the confessional in the school.

"It was January 1944; I think he was the chaplain or a visiting priest. He asked me did I have any impure thoughts, which I thought was if you wished anyone harm. Then he felt my privates in the confessional – there was a board or something I think he moved – and said if I kept having bad thoughts I would swell up there. I didn't know what he meant. I thought I was going to swell up in the confessional and die of hunger. I was given three rosaries for penance.

"While I was saying the rosary the priest was finished and he brought be up to the sacristy. He sat me on a chair and went to a side room. Then he came back and pulled a chair over right in front of me. He was wearing a long cassock. I noticed his legs were bare.

"He stood up and started fondling my privates. Then he must have masturbated and caught the semen in his hanky. Then he said if I ever did this and my white stuff went on the ground, my name would grow there and everyone who saw this would know it was me that had done this. He said it was God telling him this and I wasn't to tell anyone. He said if I told anyone the person would stone me to death."

Pat, a refined, soft-spoken man, holds his head in his hands before he recounts the story of the pommel horse.

"One evening, about 7, I had to go down near the assembly hall on the way to the toilet. I looked over and saw Brother H (as cited earlier) and Brother J (name supplied) abusing two boys on the pommel horse in the hall. I thought first it was a new exercise they were showing to the boys. But then I saw the boys' trousers were down and the Brothers were abusing the boys at each end of the pommel horse."

Pat finds the courage then to speak about what was done to him in a dormitory when he was 15. It was August 1947 in a Catholic school in the heart of the capital city of a very Catholic country.

"I was in the dormitory; we were moved there at 14. Every night, I could hear two boys a night being brought into Brother K's room (name supplied).

"You'd hear bits of whinging and crying. I was only three beds from the room. I used to pray every night he'd pass by my bed, well, I suppose that's why we're called survivors, I'd pray that it wouldn't be me. Not that I knew what was going on. But eventually I did find out. He did it to me.

"I had a bad hip because of the drillmaster kicking me. He knew I had a bad hip. I couldn't do football or hurling. He said 'be outside my room tonight. I'll massage that hip of yours.' I waited outside until about nine, wondering what was going to happen to me.

"He called me. I went in. He put me lying face down on the bed. He massaged the left side of my hip, then the right side, massaging, massaging, then this unmerciful pain. My left leg shot up. I must have kicked him. 'How dare you kick a man of the cloth,' he shouted, 'you'll suffer for this, you pup.'

"The next day I was put in a dormitory for 120 boys with three long passages; one either side, one down the middle, and I had to wax it and polish it every night for 10 nights, only Saturday I had off.

"He never did it to me again. I suppose it was the kick I gave him. But he kept taking other boys."

It should be noted here that in its investigation of Artane, the Ryan Report found in its general conclusions that "Sexual abuse of boys was a chronic problem in Artane."

While boys were brutalised physically and sexually in Artane, they were also abused mentally. "We were told that women were the personification of everything that was evil," Pat Lambert recalls, "though we didn't know what personification even meant. They made you afraid of women. They said if you went near a woman you'd got a disease and the treatment for this was gruesome."

From speaking with survivors, both men and women, it is evident that negative attitudes to the opposite sex, combined with an absence of sex education and the pervasiveness of abuse, had a profound effect on their adult lives. In many cases, those who survived childhood abuse faced a double sentence, finding only misery and loneliness in an adulthood in which lasting relationships were difficult, if not impossible, and which were invariably infused with guilt.

It took Pat Lambert 25 years to emerge from this abyss. After leaving Artane on February 24, 1948, two days short of his 16th birthday, Pat began work as a farm labourer with a family in the Midlands (Athlone). There he worked long, hard hours. His payment was "two shillings going to Mass on Sundays".

While working on the farm, he developed lameness, which he believes was caused by the beatings and by the drillmaster in Artane and probably exacerbated on the farm.

In October 1949, he was taken to the Mater Hospital in Dublin, where he had to have an operation on his hip. The surgery was uneventful but his stay in the Mater sparked a series of events that would have a dramatic effect on his life. It began with Nurse Kelly.

"Nurse Kelly, a lovely lady from Mayo, asked why I wasn't having any visitors. I told her I hadn't any family as far as I knew, according to Artane. She asked where I was born and I told her." Nurse Kelly then apparently started to take matters into her own hands.

One week before Christmas, on December 18, 1949, Pat had an unexpected visitor at the Mater. It was his sister Mary, alerted he believes by Nurse Kelly.

"I saw this woman standing at the door. She had a gap in her teeth. I thought somehow it might be Mary. She sat down. She said she was my sister, that she'd finally found me. I said a few words that I can't remember I was so amazed. We hardly had a chance for a conversation.

"Visiting time was almost up when she got to the hospital so she had to go fairly quickly but she said she'd come in with her husband before Christmas."

Pat's joy would be short-lived, however.

"Mary was no sooner gone but I was measured for a pair of crutches. One of the nurses said 'you're going for a nice drive in the morning.'" The next day Pat was taken back to Artane, on whose authority we do not know. He stayed there for one night and the next day he was sent from Artane to the Christian Brothers in Rathfarnam Castle to do house work, for which he was paid half a crown on Wednesdays.

One record shows he did well in Rathfarnam, where the following notation was made: "G. Work, G. Manner, G. Boy." But Pat himself didn't like the Brothers and soon he found a job outside Dublin, milking cows for a farmer named Charlie Byrne.

In the meantime, his sister was continuing to try to find him. When she asked the hospital where he had gone, Pat said she was told it was none of her business. But she thought otherwise. What followed was a series of Sherlockian twists.

"Mary's brother-in-law Bill Keenahan had cows and Paddy Byrne, Charlie's brother, had a lorry that used to bring Bill's milk to the dairy. Charlie also brought his own milk to the same dairy. I don't know how the conversation started, but one day Charlie happened to mention to Paddy that he had a young fella from Artane working for him. Paddy told Bill, for some reason. Then Bill told Mary."

Within minutes, Mary had made up her mind. It was only a chance but she had to try. Next day she asked her husband Alfred to tackle up the pony and trap and he and Mary travelled the eight miles or so from Lucan to Charlie Byrne's farm in Saggart.

"I remember I was milking cows and I felt this hand on my shoulder. I looked up and saw Mary standing there beside me. She asked me where I had gone and said 'now that I've found you, we'll never let those fuckers separate us again. You're coming home with us, so finish up here quickly.

"It was then I found out my family were all still alive, my mother, my brother and two more sisters. I found out our whole family was split up in the Forties, to Wexford, Carriglea and Artane and our mother was sent to the mental home for two years.

"My brother got much the same treatment at Carriglea that I got at Artane and my two sisters were abused in a convent in New Ross. Mary was in a place in Townsend St in Dublin getting injections – for what she didn't know."

Mary had traced their mother a few years earlier and suggested Pat should meet her. "I was 21 at the time. The meeting happened at a bus stop in Dublin in 1953; five years after I'd left Artane. My mother had travelled from Wexford to meet me."

The meeting was brief – and traumatic.

"When I met her, the very first thing she said was 'why didn't you answer my letters.' When I told her I'd got no letters and the Brothers told me all belonging to me were dead, she hit me across the side of the face and then the other side for 'lying', she called it, about the Christian Brothers. 'How dare you say a thing like that, lying, about those holy people,' she said.

"I remember thinking 'I don't need this'." Pat stormed off and never saw his mother again until he attended her funeral five years later, in 1958, when she died at the age of 52.

Pat found out many years later from his sister Mary that his mother had indeed written him many letters while he was in Artane. Mary had posted them from the County Home.

In 1953, Pat went to live in Dublin with Mary and her husband and remained living with them for the next seven years. In 1961, at the age of 29, he decided to try to make a fresh start in England and left for London with his brother.

Pat worked hard in London and soon found a job as a grounds man at the illustrious Queen's Tennis Club at Baron's Court, home to the British Open.

At the same time, he was enjoying London. He had been living there now for 12 years and had started to get to know his recently widowed Irish-born landlady, Gertie, encouraged by her daughter Maureen.

One evening, as the three of them were sitting around the kitchen table at the house in Shepherd's Bush, Maureen remarked that Pat and Gertie would make 'a right old married couple.' Pat decided to take the plunge. "You wouldn't marry me," he said across the table to Gertie. To his surprise and delight, she responded, "Of course, I would."

"We were married at Hammersmith registry office at half past eleven on December 23, 1974, the best day of my life." Pat was 42 and for the next 19 years, until his wife died in 1993, he experienced what he calls "the best and worst part of my life"

When his beloved wife died Pat became wracked with guilt, haunted again by the ghosts of Artane. "She was the best lady ever born. When she died of ovarian cancer, I was sure it was my fault for ages, until I got bereavement counselling because of the fear they'd beaten into us in Artane."

Even more powerful than the guilt was the raw ferocity of the loss of the woman who had given him the only love he had ever known. He was bereft without her. There was no one now to shield him from the savage nightmares of Artane.

As Christmas approached in 1993, eight months after Gertie's death, Pat tried to kill himself through carbon monoxide poisoning in his car.

The following year he attempted suicide again but pulled back from crashing his car at the last minute. "I was driving at 100 miles an hour and decided to pull into the centre of the road. I was driving at high speed. Suddenly I felt as if someone had slapped me on the face, Gertie, I suppose. I slowed down before rounding the bend and went back to the right side. I was shaking. Then I was crying. In the car that passed me, there was a man driving and I could see what must have been his three kids in the back. I could have killed them all."

The horror subsided, but not the pain. Three more suicide attempts followed over the next three years. Once he tried to drown himself in a lake but was rescued by a Dublin bus driver, who was fishing nearby on his day off.

In 1996, Pat took a drug overdose and in 1997, he pulled out in front of a large transport lorry. "Each time I was saved. I think it was Gertie looking out for me."

Over the next few years and by the time he suffered the next biggest loss in his life, the death of his sister Mary in 2009, Pat had found constructive ways to cope and respond to pain with the help of the Aislinn Centre for abuse survivors. Pat has attended the centre regularly for over a decade. "It has been my salvation," he stresses. "My salvation."

Pat Lambert's tortuous journey over seven decades is summed up, in part, on the back of a photograph that he carries in his inside pocket.

The faded black-and-white photo shows five adults standing together. Towards the centre stands the tallest, Pat. To his left are his brother John and sister Betty. To his right are his sisters Mary and Sarah. No one is smiling. On the back of the photograph, Pat has written, "August 1974. First time together since 1942."

Sometimes the clouds lift, connections are made and life can seem normal. It happens when Pat is driving. He loves to drive and each summer he travels by ferry to England and drives across the country to visit his three stepchildren and their children. In between, he keeps in close touch with his nine nephews and nieces in Ireland. One of his nieces arranged a trip for him to watch car racing at Mondello Park in Kildare on his 80th birthday. "It's only now I feel I belong to people," he says.

But such peace is fleeting. Pat Lambert has long accepted that he will never rid himself of the nightmares, of the evil inflicted on him as a boy.

"I can never see myself ever forgiving or forgetting those evil people and what those Brothers, who broke my spirit, did to me. They brutalized us. We did nothing to deserve such treatment.

"Nothing."

6

STORY OF GERRY MORAN

"I was black, my brother was white. Coloured children got hell"

A black boy and a white boy stand side by side in a First Communion photograph. They sometimes played together, even fought together, but mostly they were strangers to one another, aware only that they were growing up in the same institution.

Thirty years would pass before Gerry Moran would discover that the white boy in the Communion suit was his brother Pascal. But they would never meet again because by then, Pascal was dying in America.

"We could have been playing together, or fighting, and we never knew we were brothers," Gerry Moran says, with a mixture of anger and sadness.

"They destroyed our lives in the institutions but they stole our identity too. I never knew about him and he probably never knew about me. They gave us numbers. We were blood brothers and we never knew it.

"Yet somehow I had an idea at the back of my head; someone must have mentioned a brother. But at that stage I thought I was making it up because I thought I had no-one, I was an orphan."

Many years later, when Gerry was in his 30s, he went to a reunion of some of those who had been at St Francis Xavier Industrial School for Girls and Junior Boys, in Ballaghadereen, Co. Roscommon, and someone asked him how his brother was.

It was then he realized that he hadn't made it up. He began looking for his records and finally got his file from Ballaghadereen and found the First Communion photo showing Pascal and himself, sometime in the late 1960s.

He discovered court records showing that he and his brother had been admitted to the Ballaghadereen institution, run by the Sisters of Charity, on July 1, 1960 because his mother was "not exercising proper guardianship" and was also said to be "a woman without means."

Gerry Moran was just five months old that July in 1960; his brother Pascal was three years old.

Gerry thinks his mother, who was from Westport, Co Mayo, was "quite wild" when she was young. She had Pascal in 1957 when she was about 17 or 18. She was unmarried. Sometime after that, she left for London where, he believes, she met his father. By the time she returned to Westport in 1960, she was pregnant again.

"It must have been a big scandal. She had Pascal. Then she went to London and she became pregnant again and came home and had me, a black kid."

Over the years, Gerry continued to search for his records and finally traced his mother about 14 years ago. But she was no longer in Ireland.

He discovered she had built a new life for herself in the United States. She was now married and living in Michigan, in the heartland of America. "She's done very well for a woman without means," he says, ruefully.

They began to write to one another. She told him about Pascal. That she had left Westport for America soon after her two sons had been admitted to the industrial school in Ballaghadereen.

But another shock awaited him. And it would cut right to his core.

His mother told him that his brother was living in America too. That she had come back from America for Pascal. That she had gone to the institution for him. That she had taken him out when he was 11. That she had left Gerry behind.

"That was the worst thing," Gerry Moran says, "that she left me behind, abandoned a second time. She went to Ballaghadereen first thinking Pascal was there and then she went to Kilkenny where he'd been transferred soon after he'd made his Communion. But she left me in Ballaghadereen, never even visited me. She went back to America with Pascal and left me. I will never forgive her for that.

"The hardest thing, too, is her not explaining why. Even if she lied, that would be something. Even if she said to me the reason I took Pascal was because he was older, that would have been something."

Could it have been because Pascal was white and Gerry was black? "It could be possibly, yeah, she never mentioned that, we didn't go that far. It could have been possible. I don't even know if she was married then and if she was whether she told her husband about me or was influenced by him."

They would talk on the phone, too, very angry calls. "At the beginning they were roaring matches. I was shouting at her, asking her why this happened. She wouldn't say much. She wouldn't tell me anything about Pascal. I don't know what his life was like, nothing.

"All she'd say to me was 'my life was hard as well'. That's it. I'd love to get an explanation, but she says nothing. I don't know who Edward Moran, my father, is. I'd like to find out that."

She sent him photos of his aunts and cousins in the US, the family he never knew he had. One is a glowing picture of a family party, wide American smiles, celebratory wine glasses in hand, a well-heeled group, a world away from Westport and its secrets. He points to his mother but the others are strangers to him, as he is probably to them.

For Gerry Moran, receiving the photos was "like a punishment".

"She sent them all with no explanation and I can guarantee you none of them know about me, not one of them. Even her sister in Westport didn't know about me. I think she was the outcast of the world, the Catholic things, being pregnant, not being married, never mind a coloured kid back then. I think that was why she left."

Then one morning, about 14 years ago, his mother phoned him with news that jolted him "like a bolt of lightning".

She told him that his brother Pascal was very ill. He was in hospital. He was dying.

"She didn't give me many details about him or where he was, only that he'd been living rough in America; he'd gone through hell there, roaming about. He was on drugs. It was Aids that killed him. He was probably destroyed by what had happened to him in the institutions.

"He was dying now and part of me wanted to see him again. But at the time, I had no money to go over. Pascal died on the 14th of March 2001. He was 44.

"I never saw him before he died. That was hard. There wasn't a relationship but he was my brother. It would have been nice to have met him. He will always be in my heart because as brothers I feel we'll never be apart."

Gerry believes Pascal told his mother little or nothing about his life in the institutions. "I don't think he'd have said much to her, he'd have been too gone."

Neither has she ever asked Gerry about what happened to him.

"I'll never tell her now. I feel she's not entitled to know to be honest, she caused a lot of it; she could have made a better effort then. It's sad but I accept that's the way it'll be. I think she'll die and I'll never have seen her, that's being honest."

Today Gerry Moran, who once had a mop of thick black curls, keeps his hair tightly shaved to help him forget how a nun pulled it in the industrial school in Ballaghadereen. A few years ago, he turned his pain into verse:

"As the night lies quiet,
Fear is in the air,
Nobody attempts to speak,
Or they'll be pulled by the hair.

"My first memory would be when I was five or six and walking down to the orchard. It was a long walk, in our bare feet and if you were caught talking, you got a slap on the back of the head. If I was caught eating any apples I'd be beaten too. We'd pick apples all day and they'd sell them then.

"We had reunions, some of us, later on and I met this woman and she was in floods of tears when she saw me. She said 'I used to mind you when you were a baby'. She was about nine then. It was kids minding kids.

"She said she saw the nuns pulling me by the hair for no reason. My hair was curly and it used to stick out and they'd grab it. She was in floods of tears.

"They'd call you and if you weren't quick enough, they didn't need an excuse. It was easy; they'd grab me by the hair and pull it."

Gerry Moran points to a scar under his right eye as he recounts the terrors of bath time in Ballaghadereen when he was six years old.

"There were usually 10 of us to a bath. When I was about six or seven I was thrown into a bath of scalding hot water, I was scalded and it scarred my face. I remember all the nun on duty did was put a bit of cream on the mark. I still have the mark under my right eye.

"I remember wetting the bed and being made to stand at the end of the dormitory with the wet sheet wrapped around me. I could be left standing there for a good while. Then I would get a beating from the nun in charge of the dormitory. Sometimes she would tell us to go to the head nun for more punishment.

"They usually beat me with their hands but sometimes they used the wooden cross they were wearing around their neck."

Cruel as it was for the children in Ballaghadereen, it was even worse if you were black.

"Being black wasn't that unusual. There were a few other coloured kids there. But the coloured children got hell.

"The nuns would call us names such as "nig-nog" or "blackie". We were always left behind and other children would get picked out instead of us, when local people came in the summer to take children out on holidays. We were never put forward for this. As a result I never left the place until I was transferred out."

When Gerry started going to the local national school run by the Christian Brothers he was pleased at first. Things were bound to be better. "We thought it was great, we were actually getting away from the nuns."

But what awaited Gerry Moran at the Christian Brothers school was a worse kind of hell.

It began when he was just eight.

"I was sexually assaulted by one Brother at the school. I was about eight. It happened in the classroom in the school, usually on a Friday evening after school.

"The Brother would ring the nuns and tell them I'd be late back. Then he'd feel me up and would force me to masturbate him, he'd fondle me; he'd ejaculate. He'd give me a few sweets after this."

Such assaults occurred as often as the Christian Brother got a chance. All it took was a call to the nuns to say he'd be "late back."

"It happened to me five or six times. At the time, I knew something wasn't right, but I didn't know what. I didn't say anything to the nuns because I was afraid of being beaten. I had no one to turn to. We never could open our mouths to the nuns in case we got hit."

It was the perfect environment for savagery: children with no one to turn to, cut off by fear. Anyone could do whatever they liked, whenever they liked, wherever they liked to the children, like Gerry, who had been put in their care by the courts of the Irish State.

No one ever came to see Gerry Moran in Ballaghadereen in the long years from the age of five months to nine years old. Not his mother. Not his grandmother, who'd delivered him. Not his father. Not his four aunts. Nor did he ever get to travel back to Westport to see them.

"Many of the kids in that place went home during the holidays. We didn't even know when it was Christmas. We were orphans. We couldn't understand why we were left behind. So they could do what they liked to us."

In 1969, Gerry Moran was turning nine. Unknown to him, events were unfolding that year that would plunge his young life into greater turmoil.

The decision had been made to close the industrial institution because of declining vocations to the Sisters of Charity – two years later the order left Ballaghadereen to be replaced by the Sisters of Mercy, who subsequently ran St Francis Xavier School until 1992.

The closure of the industrial institution in 1969, however, must have been a momentous event for the Sisters of Charity. Nearly a century of history was drawing to a close. They had come to Ballaghadereen in 1874, led by Mother Agnes Morragh-Bernard of Cheltenham, England, who would later found Foxford Woollen Mills. Shortly after arriving, the Sisters set up St Francis Xavier' School and in the late 1880s the MP for East Mayo successfully petitioned the Commons in London to locate an industrial school at the convent. Now, 80 years later, this industrial institution was finally closing.

The impending closure after so many years in Ballaghadereen must undoubtedly have sparked much discussion both within the order and locally. However, as Gerry Moran recalls, the children in the institution itself were told nothing about the plan to close it. Neither were they told anything about where they were going, nor what might happen to them there.

"The day we were told we were all leaving Ballaghadereen, we thought we were going home. Little did we know, we were on our way to yet another industrial school."

The girls went to Benada Abbey in Ballymote, Co. Sligo, also run by the Sisters of Charity, the boys to Artane in Dublin, run by the Christian Brothers, and some, like Pascal and Gerry, to Mount Carmel in Moate, Co Westmeath, run by the Sisters of Mercy. However, soon afterwards Pascal was transferred to St Joseph's in Kilkenny, which, like Ballaghadereen, was run by the Sisters of Charity. "I now know Pascal went through hell there," Gerry says.

What this "hell" may have been like was revealed in 2009 in the Ryan Report. Referring to St Josephs' it says: *"It was dogged at two separate periods in its history by serious instances of sexual abuse and the Congregation did not deal with these appropriately or with the children's best interests in mind."* The periods referred to were in 1954 and in the 1970s.

The physical abuse that Gerry had suffered in Ballaghaderreen was even more severe in Moate.

"I remember one nun (whom he names) I'd describe as a bad person. She was a big physical nun. She'd often beat me just for the sake of it with whatever she could lay her hand on.

"She'd usually call me into the kitchen for the beating. She'd often hit me with her knuckles, with the hand she wore her ring on. I'd be playing football in the yard and on a few occasions broke the window. She'd come out and drag me in and beat me. I remember her hitting me with the ring so hard and it broke my two front teeth. I had to go to the dentist that time.

"One day, when I was cleaning the fire in the main convent, a nun (whom he names) hit me with a poker across my head; I hadn't been cleaning the fire quickly enough for her. I was 11 or 12 at the time. It started to bleed. I have a scar on my head since."

His is scarred too by a nightmare surrounding the fate of two boys.

"In the morning the bell would ring to wake us up. All the boys would jump up. Once the nun entered the room, everyone was on alert. We were all terrified of her. But two boys stayed in bed and never moved. I think to this day, those two boys were dead because we never saw them again. She (the nun) cleared the room immediately when she saw the two boys were not stirring. I was about 11 or 12 at the time. Till the day I die, that memory will stay with me. "

Questions about the disappearance of some children from industrial institutions and whether they could have died, haunt other survivors too. On the second day of the Dáil debate on the Ryan Report, on June 12, 2009, the Minister of State at the Department of Finance, Martin Mansergh, told the chamber, "There were a number of unexplained deaths in the Irish (industrial school) situation."

A related question on whether the number of deaths within these institutions was higher than among the cohort population outside was also raised in the Staines report for the Ryan Commission. Entitled, *An Assessment of the Health Status of Children detained at Irish Industrial Institution 1940 to 1983*, it concluded:

> *"There is no indication of any excess mortality, but given the many uncertainties, especially in the population at risk, we cannot be certain about this."*

Such uncertainty is very troubling for survivors. Equally troubling is the fact that it is impossible to measure the full extent of the impact the abuse had on the level of suicide and premature deaths among survivors. Gerry Moran recalls one such premature death.

Referring to a much-feared nun in Ballaghadereen, he says: "We were all scared of that nun. It gave her power. She feared anyone who stood up to her. She got rid of one boy to Letterfrack. I found out that having spent years in and out of prison he died in the street in Dublin. He just gave up and died. He was only 42. All this because of what they did to him."

In this context, it should be noted that under *Effects on adult life*, the Ryan Report stated:

> *"Most witnesses reported life-long negative effects and damaging physical, psychological, and social consequences of childhood abuse in Schools. The legacy of alcohol abuse, depression, physical and verbal aggression, anger, lack of trust, and social isolation was evident in the accounts provided by many witnesses about their adult lives."*

Gerry Moran ran away from Moate four or five times with a few other boys but each time, the Gardaí caught them.

"The Gardaí would call the convent and a nun would come and collect us. Then we'd get a severe beating with whatever came to hand, a favourite was a ruler on the back of the knuckles."

One escape bid was particularly daring. It was the time he went to see his friend Ruth L, who had been transferred from Ballaghaderreen to Benada Abbey about four year earlier. Gerry was determined to see Ruth again and managed to travel halfway across the country from Westmeath to Benada Abbey in Sligo to see her.

"I got lifts on the road and then I got all the way to the girls dormitory before I was caught. The nun caught me under Ruth's bed; can you imagine me, 14 or 15? She called the police. They rang the police in Moate."

Gerry would suffer severely for this transgression.

"In Moate, the nun was waiting, enraged. She had a belt and she flogged me with it. Froth came out of her mouth. She was a vicious nun.

"Another time a few of us ran away while the nuns were on retreat. We were taken back by the guards. She flogged us. That nun put the fear of God into all of us, even years later we feared her."

"She'd use a wooden spoon on your knuckles. Sometimes she'd use her beads over the back of the head. She had a ring on her finger. She'd use that too. If you were scrubbing the floor and you weren't doing it fast enough, she'd slap you. She'd come behind you and slap you hard."

Years later, long after the boys had left Moate and grown to adulthood, the fear of this nun still haunted them.

"I got a phone call when she died and we all went down (to Moate), we were adults then. To make sure it was her who was dead, because the fear was still there. About 20 or 30 of us went down. We took one look into the coffin and we were gone. As adults after all those years the fear was still there."

When Gerry Moran went to Moate about 18 years ago, he found the industrial school had been knocked down, though the convent was left. "With it the secrets were gone too. No-one could come down and say this happened to me there and so on."

Gerry got his first job at the local Snowcream dairy factory, and stayed in the convent for another year while working at Snowcream. "I'd get my meals at the convent. I thought I'd die an old man there. It was the only system I knew.

"Then I got involved with people in the town. I got into trouble, I started drinking and fighting, robbing a few places in the town. And of course, everyone knew it was me. I was very wild when I was in Moate. I hated the system. I hated everyone."

Once he robbed Snowcream. When he was getting his wages, he grabbed a bunch of other wages from the table too.

"They started screaming. I ran out. There was a bus coming. I got to Dublin. I realized I had money but I didn't know what to do with it. I didn't pay the B&B and the guards caught me and sent me back to Moate, then to the court to be charged. I was put on probation. I knew I had to leave Moate."

Gerry Moran was now 17 years old but the institutions had left him totally ill-equipped for adulthood in every way, mentally, emotionally.

When he left Moate, he went to Dublin again. He lived on the streets for a couple of days. "I didn't really care. They'd told me I was no use. I actually believed it for a long time, that I was no use.

"I got odd jobs, cleaning jobs. That's all I thought I could get. No decent jobs."

Then he heard about a friend from Moate who was in Dublin and he tracked him down. He was in luck. His friend had a flat and Gerry stayed with him for a while.

He told Gerry about signing on for social welfare. "He knew the ins and outs. I knew nothing. I was like someone out of Mars. This guy was a bright kid. He went on to college. He became a teacher."

But soon Gerry slipped into crime. "I was in and out of prison". But all the time he kept in touch with his friend and one day he met his fiend's sister. Soon they would fall in love.

"She's the mother of my kids (three daughters and now three grandchildren). She was a survivor as well. That's why I thought that we could get on but it didn't happen that way." However, Gerry sees his kids all the time and is close to them.

"I thought I'd be dead and gone by the time I was 20, the way I was going. I was going nowhere: drinking, into crime, in and out of prison. There was nothing then, no centre like the Aislinn Centre for survivors. The worst thing was, there was no one to talk to. That was the worst. I'd go into a pub, sit in a corner on my own and just drink."

Gerry Moran decided to go to London, like thousands of other survivors before him, leaving his partner and his two-year-old daughter behind. He hoped to find a job, to get away from the pain, to make thinks work. By now, he was nearly 29.

"I was going to start all over again. I was on the boat and I had one pound in my pocket. That was it."

In London, he found help again from his friend, who had moved there a few years earlier. "I stayed with him. But it wasn't going to work. I was there with my cans. He was there with his books. I was drinking from my cans and he was studying his books. I knew I was only getting in his way."

Then one day, Gerry's partner and his daughter arrived in London. "We had another child. We thought it would work out but it didn't.

"I was drinking, not coming home. It was bad. There was a gang of us going around together. She was supposed to understand because she was a survivor. Things were dire. The kids would ask me to read a bedtime story or help with their homework. I couldn't do it."

He stayed in London for about 18 months and then decided to return to Dublin. But he drifted in and out of crime. "I had no confidence, no faith in myself and I'd always been rebellious."

All the time he was haunted by his torment in the institutions and by unanswered questions.

About 10 years ago, when Gerry was in his 40s, he travelled to Westport to try to find out about his mother. He met her sister. "I didn't know what way she was going to react to me. I went down. I knocked on the door. There was no answer." A neighbour said he should try the pub. "I thought hang on, it's only 11 in the morning, but I went down anyway. "

There in the pub he found his aunt. He told her who he was, but she had apparently never heard of her sister's son. "She gave the impression at first she didn't know, I don't know whether she did or not. Then she hugged me, she was very nice. I didn't ask her about Pascal."

She told Gerry about his mother and his grandmother, and how they'd lived in rooms below the courthouse.

It evoked a chilling image for Gerry Moran. "That means you could be getting sent away in the courtroom for 10 years and the family could be living in another part of the courthouse. I couldn't believe it until I saw it for myself when I went to Westport."

She told Gerry that a week to 10 days after the court order sending him and Pascal to Ballaghaderreen his mother left Westport for America.

After a few years, she met a man over there and married him. Her husband is now dead and she's living in Michigan. His aunt told him that his mother had come back to Westport a number of times since, sometimes once or twice a year in recent years. There were family photos to prove it.

But Gerry Moran is in none of the photos, his existence as deftly airbrushed from them as it had been from the US photos.

"It proves to me she never wanted to see me, she'd no intention of seeing me. If she'd wanted to, she'd have made the effort.

He hasn't travelled over to America to see her either. "I'd probably like to see her but the thing is does she want to see me?"

Their letters to one another are devoid of warmth or emotion. "Hers are basic and I keep mine basic too". She never asks about her grandchildren. They never ask about her. She's got three great-grandkids and she knows nothing about them

"She came back once. She took Pascal. She left me. I don't think I can ever forgive her for that. She could easily have taken me as well, saved me from another nine years of that terror."

Such abandonment will always anger him but it is not that that has shattered Gerry Moran's life. "That was nothing compared to the things that happened later on. What the nuns did and what the Brothers did."

Not only to him but to his friends, some who survived, others who did not. One friend from Moate, who was in and out of prison, died on the streets in Dublin. "He gave up. It was his way out. He was only 52 when he died."

He visits another friend in Mountjoy prison. He's been there over 16 years for manslaughter. "It could easily have happened to me if I got into a fight. He believes he's in prison all these years because of being in the industrial schools.

"They don't realize the damage they caused. The long-term damage is unbelievable. Marriages, everything, there's nothing it didn't affect.

"They got away with it. Some are dead but others aren't. They were never named and shamed in the Ryan Report. It would have taken a lot of the pain and hurt away if these nuns and brothers had been named and shamed."

But for Gerry Moran there is victory in survival, motivation even. "Surviving was me not giving in to them. Because if I died, they would have won.

"As I get older I'm calmer. You learn to move on a bit. The Aislinn Centre continues to help me. But the terror never leaves me, never.

"And it probably killed Pascal."

Irish Examiner

Thursday, May 21, 2009   www.irishexaminer.com   No. 58,111   €1.80 / Stg £1.10

CHILD ABUSE REPORT

SHATTERED LIVES

The worst was seeing a young boy die. He was 12 years old ... he was beaten by brothers on the landing and he fell over the banister

I found a little girl dead in her bed after they'd gone for a walk and the girl hadn't been feeling up to it

I overheard someone say that my mother had died the night before. When I asked about it I was ignored and dismissed

We were all lined up naked and slapped in the face a lot. We had to drink water from toilets and were all washed in the same bath water

I was beaten and hospitalised by the head brother and not allowed to go to my father's funeral in case my bruises were seen

I was beaten until knocked out and my head split. My finger was placed in boiling water until all feeling was lost

I was stripped naked by a nun and beaten with a stick and given no supper and humiliated

When I told nuns about being molested by an ambulance driver, I was stripped and whipped to 'get the devil out of you'

At six, I was raped by a nun and at 10 I was hit with a poker on the head by a nun

I was left out in the cold one winter and stayed near the boiler where older boys tried to molest me and I had to fight them off

I was tied to a cross and raped whilst others masturbated at the side

I can take any abuse, but the worst thing was having no one. I was told my parents were dead. I found out in my 50s they were alive

Night-times were the worst; if you weren't taken out of bed and beaten you were listening to it happening to someone else

I wouldn't stop crying. I was down in the ground. The first thing he could lay his hand on was a hammer and he hit me and damaged me

They would check your underwear and if they were soiled you would get whacked for it with a hand brush, 21 times

I'll never forget the cat-o'-nine-tails. Observing other boys stripped and the blood running down as they were being flogged

I was beaten stark naked for wetting the bed, two or three different people would beat me. They liked beating kids naked

In the classroom he threw me out the window because I soiled myself. He was a bully, he hit me with the leather on the hands

One new lad covered himself getting dressed. This Brother decided he was going to make a man out of him and pulled off his clothes

Irish Examiner front page on the Ryan Report

(Press Association)

(The Irish Times)

Solidarity March June 10, 2009

(Press Association)

Christine Buckley addressing Solidarity March

(Press Association)

7

STORY OF ELLEN GUINAN

"My father had all these Georgian houses yet six of us were put away"

Ellen Guinan was born 87 years ago into a wealthy family in Dublin, where her father owned a string of Georgian houses, five cottages, two stables and a large hardware shop. She was an unlikely candidate for an industrial institution and today she still manages to smile at the contradiction, even as she grapples with the mystery.

Her face is lined a little now, but it is not an old face. It sparkles with a smile when she recalls that her birth date in 1927 was the 23rd of June, breaking into the words of *Spancil Hill*.

It being the 23rd of June, the day before the fair,
When Ireland's sons and daughters and friends assembled there,
The young, the old, the brave and the bold their duty to fulfil,
At the little church in Clooney, a mile from Spancil Hill.

She smiles again as she finishes the verse. "I enjoy a bit of fun. It's what's kept me going." For 87 years, she says, and against the odds.

Ellen's life started well. Her father, an English Protestant, born in Lancaster in 1874, owned four leasehold Georgian houses in Dublin and five cottages, which he rented out.

He also had a large hardware shop and stables in the city, on Harmony Row, near the family home.

"There were nine of us in the family, four brothers and five sisters. The eldest was born in 1919 and there was about two years between us all."

Then one spring morning, in February 1934, four months before Ellen turned seven, the family was rent asunder.

"At that time, being a child, I didn't know my father had all this property. It wasn't until later in life, when I grew up, I knew this and I was saying to myself, Why? Why? He had all this and six of us were put away."

Her father died aged 62, in January 1936, two years after Ellen, her two younger sisters and three older brothers had been committed to industrial schools.

"I didn't see the boys being taken away but I found out years later that they were taken to St Saviours in Dominick St (Dublin) just before us.

"My sister Margaret was working in Jacobs, so she was left at home, and my brother and my other sister were just babies so they were lucky enough to escape too. We were the unlucky ones."

Their committal to industrial schools was apparently carried out on their father's instructions. He had developed kidney failure and Ellen believes that splitting up the family was his idea and she blames his sisters, who were living in Dublin, for "taking everything" after her father died.

"They went to court and got the houses after my father died. A landlord took over and my mother had to pay rent."

Legal documents, dated 16 April 1936, name her father's two sisters and confirm that they did indeed take over all his property after he died.

The documents themselves are a window into Georgian Dublin in the 1930s. Among the effects listed in them are: "An ice cream pony car complete with equipment £8; a pony £5; iron copying press 5 shillings; mahogany sideboard £3; piano old and defective £1.10.0; chiffonier mirror back £6.10.0; grandfather clock £5; writing case, small, 3 shillings" and onwards through the minutiae that made up the life of this relatively well-to-do family.

Thus, three months after her father had died, his properties and every item of value within them were sold by his sisters but neither Ellen's mother, nor any of his nine children benefited.

It came as a dreadful shock, decades later, when Ellen found out why her mother had little legal protection against the move.

The answer came in the 1911 census. One day, as Ellen was poring over the census for clues, she could hardly believe what she discovered. She found out that her father had been married—but not to her mother.

"I was well into my Sixties when I discovered this. I couldn't believe it.

"Then I began to piece it together. The census confirmed the bits of information I'd gathered over the years. I didn't begin to put two and two together until after my mother died in 1966." It was then that her mother's sister told Ellen the story of Ester, her father's wife, a story she'd now confirmed in the 1911 census.

"I'd often heard bits about Ester and wondered who she was. I thought she might have been a cousin or a neighbour. It was my Aunt Ba who told me. She said my father married Ester, probably around the turn of the century, soon after he arrived in Dublin.

"He'd wanted sons but she couldn't have children so he left Ester and went to live with my mother — this must have been sometime between the 1911 census and 1919 because my sister Margaret was the eldest of the nine of us and she was born that year.

"It wasn't until I saw the census showing Ester as his wife that I really knew. So when he died that's why everything went to his sisters. Ester must have been already dead."

The fact that his sisters became the trustees of his estate does tend to confirm that Ester must almost certainly have died before him. However, for reasons still unknown, Ellen's father failed to make a will that would have protected Ellen's mother and his nine children.

Ellen often wonders what became of Ester. "I feel a bit sorry for her. The census said they were married 19 years. It must have been hard for her. My father left her and then had the nine of us with my mother.

"My sister Margaret remembers that Essie, that's what they called her, used to go into my father's shop and she felt sorry for her. I feel sorry for her too. It must have been hard for her knowing her husband had left her and had all these children with my mother."

Ellen knows from photos that her mother, then only in the late teens, must have been very attractive when she first met the Englishman, who was then in his 40s.

Her mother and father lived together in the family home from the time Margaret was born and it was at that address that he died in 1936, according to his death certificate.

Knowing his wife was dead, Ellen's father must have feared his sisters would "take everything" after he died yet he felt too powerless or weak or inept to do much about it.

His feeble solution for six of his children was the industrial institutions, while his wife ended up paying rent to a new landlord after his sisters sold his properties.

Today, 80 years later, Ellen is still trying to find answers and she is still very angry at her father. Yet it was to her father that the little seven-year-old girl called out for help when a nun physically assaulted her at St Anne's Industrial School for Girls in Booterstown, Co. Dublin, run by the Sisters of Mercy.

Ellen vividly remembers the day in 1934, two years before her father died, when she and her five siblings were taken to the institutions.

She remembers it was spring. It was a sunny afternoon. It was the perfect weather for a little girl of almost seven to play outside.

"I remember the day I was taken away. It was a sunny afternoon and I was out playing. I was roamer. I was always outside playing."

Ellen was still playing outside with her sisters when two women approached the house. She didn't take much notice of the women. She was having too much fun playing.

But the arrival of the two women was about to change this little girl's world forever. It would be rent asunder with lightning speed and brutal force and this would be the last day that Ellen and her sisters would ever play together again.

"No-one said anything to us. One minute, we were playing and the next minute, we were on this tram. I just remember being taken up the street by these two women and onto the tram.

"It was afterwards my mother's sister Ba told me that when they took us away my mother was crying. 'Oh my girls, my girls,' she was screaming. She was calling out for us.

"There was my sister Bridget, my sister Mary, and myself. The two women came down to my mother's place and took us three girls away. I was screaming and they got me onto the tram. But I managed to get off. I was running and they caught me. They dragged me back onto the tram. I was screaming 'I want to go home, I want to go home.'

"Bridget was clinging to me. Mary was in the other woman's arms." Bridget was just six years old, that day in 1934 as she clung to her sister Ellen, and Mary, now being held tightly in the stranger's arms, was just four years old.

"We got off at a station – I discovered later it was Blackrock – and up a big avenue (Booterstown). We went through these big iron gates. We were taken in and inspected. I found notes in the order's archives later describing us. They said I had a snub nose and that I was very intelligent but wilful. That day, we were all absolutely terrified when we arrived there.

"This nun then took us to the Reverend Mother who gave us the institutional clothes. I wanted to be home, I was crying. I was roaring 'I want to go home'. My sisters, too, were sobbing."

"Then they fed us. We got bread and butter and a tin mug of cocoa. But we never had enough to eat there. I was always hungry. We used to steal bread from the kitchen and they'd beat you if they caught you.

"The next day we were put in school. It was unreal; it was a strange place. We were only small. We were looking up at these people. We didn't know who they were."

The sisters had lost their family and their home. Now they would lose their names.

Like most institutionalised children, their names were replaced with numbers. "My number was 55, Bridget was 67, and Mary was 19. They'd seldom use your name. They'd just call you by your number."

"We got a basic education – reading, writing and sums though I don't remember doing any primary cert – but sometimes we'd be taken out of class and put to do the laundry and other jobs."

Ellen was then about seven-and-a-half. "There was a big school laundry and big wooden tubs and we'd be washing sheets. Our hands were small and we'd be trying to wring out the sheets. It was very hard and we'd be there for most of the day."

But worse still were the frequent beatings.

"I remember the big stick with the handles and you could hear the swish, swish of the stick. You'd hold out your hands. And they'd whack you over the legs too."

Another harrowing memory centres on an incident in a cloakroom. It was there that Ellen cried out in vain for her father to protect her.

"Children would be brought down to the cloakroom, thrown over a stepladder, knickers pulled down and then the beating would start. You'd hear the girls screams if you were passing, you could hear them crying and screaming.

"Once it happened to me. When I was seven-and-a-half or eight, it was really for nothing because we didn't commit any crime. Just doing what children do. You might talk and there was a big notice up on the stairs, SILENCE and if you whispered something, they beat you.

"I was crying; I was calling for my father, 'Oh Daddy, Daddy'. I ran out sobbing from that place."

But three-quarters of a century later, it is not her own suffering but that of her sister that still torments Ellen.

Bridget was not yet seven when she was savagely beaten for showing her father the bruises on her back.

Ellen's eyes are moist and a shiver runs through her frail, 87-year-old body as she recalls what happened to her sister once their father had left.

"My father came to see us once and they (the nuns) were in the room and my father had us around him and Bridget showed him her back where she had been beaten. When my father saw her bruising, he went ballistic. He went mad. He was ranting and raving at the nuns.

"When my father had gone, Sister C, she was evil, she had Bridget in the washroom and she nearly killed her with the beating she got.

"Beatings were usually in the cloakroom but Sister C couldn't wait to take her there. The washroom was near the visiting room so she took her there. It was horrendous, the beating she got. She was black and blue. It stayed with me all my life."

Bridget and Ellen were in the same class at school and at night were in the Sacred Heart dormitory, but Mary was in Our Lady's dormitory so they hardly ever saw their small sister.

Ellen's instinct was to look after her younger sister, Bridget. But for that, she would suffer even more.

"I have to protect my sister, I said, and they'd get after me because I was protecting Bridget from the beatings.

"I remember one day we were down at St Teresa's. It was a room at the end of the schoolyard, there were benches and there was a stage there.

"For some reason they had a class down there this day and it was geography and I was sitting on the front row and I had Bridget beside me. She used to be terrified. She was always terrified of the nuns.

"The nun said to her where is the source of the Shannon River and Bridget was terrified. She said the first thing that came into her mind and she said Wicklow. And with that the nun was coming at her and I got up and I sat on my sister's lap and the nun was telling me to get off her, get off, sit back down, sit there.

"And I said No, No. I was getting sense. My brain was kicking in, saying this isn't right. This is NOT right. So I sat on my sister and of course, I got the beatings, cross my back, cross my legs, she was in a temper, in such a temper that the spittle was coming out her mouth, and I ran on the stage and ran around and I kept shouting 'murder, murder'. She left the room. I think she realised she'd gone too far.

"I was expecting that the Reverend Mother would send for me. But nothing came of it, I was never sent for. The nun knew she'd gone too far. I had marks on my legs, everywhere. That woman didn't know when to stop."

Another memory is still raw, as Ellen recalls it vividly over 70 years later. It was the day she punched in the face and got a black eye.

"It was at Catechism class. The teacher had asked about Moses. They had pictures in this book and they had one of Moses, and you could see Moses with the Ten Commandments. The teacher was telling us things about Moses.

"The girl who sat next to me never paid attention, and this day after the lessons on Moses the nun picked on her and said 'can you tell me anything about Moses'.

"The girl was looking at the picture of Moses for a bit and then said 'Moses was the man with the big, long beard'. Of course, I started to laugh and the next minute I got a punch in the face.

"A few days later, one of the nuns came into the dining room and said they were going to Inchicore (in Dublin) to the grotto and she said, looking at me, 'you stay back'. I was the only one who didn't go. It was because I had a black eye. I must have been 11 or 12 then."

When Ellen's mother visited her, she had two schools to go to. One month she would visit Ellen and her sisters and the next month she would visit the boys. "That's when I knew the three boys were in institutions too. She'd visit them and then she'd visit us the following month."

Her mother would stay for about an hour. All the girls who had visitors would be together in one room. Ellen did manage to tell her mother about some of the physical abuse "but I got the feeling that she didn't want to know. There was nothing there between us, especially me. She never liked me. I don't know why, I suppose I was more like my father."

Her father suffered kidney failure and back then, there was no dialysis. "The cure was boiled chicken and barley water, and of course that wasn't going to cure him.

"He realised that he was dying and he had too many of us so they decided six of us would have to go. My sister Margaret also blamed a priest from Westland Row for separating us. My father and the priest wanted it and my mother didn't stand up to them."

Two years after entering the institution, Ellen learned that her father had died. "My father had visited just once. In 1936, my mother came up and told us our father had died. We didn't know what he died from then. We'd almost forgotten what he looked like. We never cried. I remember he was tall, 6ft 4in, with sandy-coloured hair. Before we went into the institution I remember him one time going into the shop, it was Halloween, and getting a big bag full of apples and oranges and sweets. I remember too, he used to bring home bowls of ice cream he'd made in the shop. Sometimes, he'd bring us out on the pony and trap and show us Dublin. When we were tired, he'd always sing, "Show me the way to go home; I'm tired and I want to go to bed." I remember him for that. After that he just fades."

Once, Ellen was hoping for a letter from her mother and when she saw some letters in a hall at the institution, she checked the names quickly in case one was for her. This simple act brought dire consequences.

"The nun (Sister M) saw me and shouted at me and told me 'I want to see you in the dining room after breakfast. You're to stay back'.

"So I stayed back. She had this stick. It wasn't smooth. It had things sticking out of it. She said hold out your hand and she came down on my hand with the stick. And now, she says, hold out the other one."

But this time, in an instant, courage became stronger than fear. Ellen decided to fight back. She was now almost 16 and would be leaving the institution soon anyway.

Or so she thought.

"The nun had the stick up and I jumped up and caught it and I pulled her down onto the floor. I got her. She met her match. I just stood there. That was it. She'd met her match. She called me a blaggard and said that from now on, I would eat my meals on my own in the scullery." But a much worse punishment was being planned for Ellen's defiance.

"A few weeks later I was sent for to go to the Reverend Mother. She told me to get my clothes and my coat. It was a brown coat, a pair of ankle sock and sandals. A nun came into the room and she said I was to go with her. The nuns wanted to get rid of me. I was setting a bad example. One minute I was there and next minute I was gone. I never had a chance to say goodbye to my sisters. I was worried about them all the time without me there to protect them.

"The nun brought me to Westland Row station (Dublin) and put me on a train. I had nothing, no luggage; just what I stood up in was all I had. She put me on a train and said there would be somebody to meet me in Athlone. I was met in Athlone by another nun. And I was taken to work in a laundry. It was about 1944 and I was coming up to 16 years of age, I should have been let out, but they sent me to the laundry, St Gabriel's laundry at the industrial school in Athlone. That was my punishment."

By this time, some of Ellen's brothers had begun working and her mother decided she could afford to take Bridget and Mary out of the industrial school. But not Ellen. "Soon after I was sent to Athlone, she took them out. But not me," Ellen says, adding, bluntly, "She never liked me."

Life in St Gabriel's laundry was tough, hot and seemingly relentless. "I worked in the laundry room from early morning till six in the evening. It was a huge hot room, full of steam and there were irons all along the walls for the shirts. I'd never seen so many irons and huge rollers that you'd feed the sheets into. You were on the floor, standing from eight to six in the evening, with half an hour for lunch.

"The girls there were mostly youngish, 16 to 20. No one could get away. We had no money. How could you leave? They had us every way. We never got paid. They were making the money. We got nothing. We lived over the laundry. We came down for breakfast and then down to the laundry. We did tablecloths, pillow cases, sheets, everything, every day. On Saturdays, we'd sweep up all around the machine.

"We had Saturday afternoon off but we had no money. Down in Athlone, we'd see the people with their kids having ice cream, but we could get nothing, so we just sat there on the banks of the Shannon.

"In the laundry there was a mad nun. When you were ironing, she had a big scissors and she'd come behind you and play games, pretending to zip your hair. I had lovely black hair and she was behind me one day. I said yes Sister, I turned and she mooched off. She always had a scissors and I was terrified she'd grab me and cut it all off."

By now, Ellen had been working in the laundry for about nine months. She began to fear that she might never get out. But once again, courage overcame fear.

"I wasn't sure it'd work, but I wrote to my mother and I told her my legs were all swollen up because we were standing all day. I said I wanted to get out. I asked one of the men on the laundry van pick-up to post the letter. He was John Joe Fitzpatrick and he put a stamp on it, God bless his heart." It worked.

"One day, a few weeks after I'd sent the letter, one of the nuns told me I was leaving. She took me to Athlone and put me on the train to Dublin. I was glad to leave the laundry but at that stage, I didn't feel anything, I was emotionally numb. It was terrible what the nuns did to people there. It was horrendous in that laundry. I was lucky to get out. Many women didn't."

Ellen thinks her mother agreed to take her home "possibly because I was old enough to work".

"When I got to Westland Row (in Dublin) I knew my way home. I took the slipway from the station to Harmony Row. When I walked in my mother said nothing but Sarah and Michael said, 'Who's that?' and then my mother said, 'That's your sister.' I was like a stranger to the three left at home. Sarah was only two when I left. Michael was only born a few months after I left. Margaret was working so I suppose my mother could afford to keep them. It was a pity she didn't keep us all. Three were left at home and six of us were taken. It was us six who were born at the wrong time.

"A bit later one of my brothers was over from England. He bought me a coat; it was a royal blue coat. It was the first decent thing that I ever had. I wore it and I wore it. Another brother came over another time and brought me a brick red coat. After a while, I got a job in a nursing home in Baggot St (Dublin) and I worked there for about two years. I was paid 8 shillings and sixpence a week. My mother took the 8 shillings off me and gave me just the sixpence. She had to feed the other four and pay rent."

Then Ellen decided to make daring move.

The Second World War had just ended and England was getting ready to embark on a huge reconstruction effort. Ellen heard that Ministry of Labour officials from England were in Dublin looking for workers, including cleaners and childminders. She went for an interview and got the job.

"I got a notice and a ticket paid and I was told I was going to Bristol and someone would be there to pick me up. I was sent to work in hostel-type accommodation – it was a huge house where women who worked for the Ministry of Labour stayed. The women went out to work in the Ministry each morning and we cleaned and so on.

"We had evenings off. They had a cook in the house so we had no work in the kitchen. I had freedom and money in my pocket. We'd go off on Sundays dancing. I had lots of boyfriends." Among them, one became special. "We met in 1950. We courted for a while and then got married in Kent; we had a grand wedding"

Ellen and her husband, who is now deceased, had two children. Their son is now a magistrate in England and their daughter is living in Dublin. Ellen and her husband came back to Dublin about seven years after their marriage when Ellen's mother was very ill.

"She treated me with total indifference but I was at her bedside when she died in St Mary's hospital in Dublin in 1966. I had my daughter with me; she was about four. 'I want to see my gran,' she said. Then my mother put her hand up and touched my daughter's head. 'You're a lovely little girl,' she said. That was at five to three. At three she died. Perhaps she was reaching me through her.

"My mother never told me anything, she wasn't warm. There was no intimacy, nothing between us; she kind of shut herself off. My daughter and I are close; I didn't want ever to repeat how my mother treated me. I suppose I blame the two of them, more my father than her, for what happened but I wouldn't be angry. I feel sorry for the pair of them, I suppose. Women were under the thumb of the man then. She was weak. She never stood up for herself.

"My father seemed a good person and maybe if he'd been in good health we'd never have been put in those hellholes, I'm giving him that much, but he should have made a will. If I could bring them back, I'd sit them down and say tell me why it happened. You had all these houses, what were you thinking about?"

Surely, she says, he could never have known what those places were really like.

"Those industrial schools were like clubs for paedophiles. Children were abused sexually and mentally and when they married, many were never happy. Their lives were destroyed. Women's lives and men's lives.

"The brain is the first computer, and it's the best. You remember where you were born, where you went to school, who your friends were. But our childhood was taken from us. The beatings, that laundry, these memories never leave you. Even if you were given the world as a present – the memories of those years still would never leave you. But you try to let the good times carry you. If you didn't you'd be depressed all the time, you'd be on drugs.

"Or maybe you wouldn't be here at all."

8

STORY OF TESSIE MULLANEY

"Three years old: fit for industrial training"

The town of Thurles, nestled in the heart of Tipperary's Suir Valley, must have looked particularly beautiful that summer morning in July 1950 as District Justice Gleeson set out for court. Awaiting his arrival there is three-year-old Tessie Mullaney, known today as the *"defendant"*.

The *"charge"* facing the three-year-old defendant is that she is destitute, the court papers tell us.

We also learn that Tessie Mullaney is *"illegitimate"* and that her mother, once a Cumann na mBan member, is now living and working in the local County Home and struggling unsuccessfully to make ends meet.

We learn, too, that Tessie has a nine-year-old sister, Mary, though she barely knows her. Two months after Tessie was born Mary was committed to an industrial school at the age of six because her mother was *"in poor circumstances financially"*. Mary had already started school at the local Presentation Convent but, nevertheless, on the morning of 8th August 1947, she was committed to the institution from the same courthouse where Tessie now awaited her own fate, on July 5, 1950.

There is no record to show whether Justice Gleeson was taken aback that morning by any of these details. But it appears more likely from the court records that the case of Tessie Mullaney was simply another routine case to be handled as expeditiously as possible.

Before noon was done on that July day in Thurles, Justice Gleeson had pronounced the three-year-old defendant *"fit for industrial training"* and had sentenced her to be *"detained"* in an industrial school for the next 13 years of her life.

Tessie Mullaney has suffered much in the intervening years but today, 64 years later, it is the sight of the notation *"fit for industrial training"* at the age of three that brings tears to her eyes and a horror that is palpable. "I suppose I shouldn't be shocked," she says, pointing to the four handwritten words, "but it still gets to me."

She does not remember who was with her in the courtroom that morning when she was thus declared *"fit for industrial training"* and given 13 years detention. Mercifully, she can recall nothing of that day. But we do know from the court records that her mother was not with her because Justice Gleeson heard that Mary Mullaney was in the County Home in Thurles from where, we are told, she had *"consented to her daughter's committal."*

The *"complainant"* in the case against the three-year-old *"defendant"* is one John Hamilton, Inspector of the National Society for the Prevention of Cruelty to Children.

He describes the reasons why the three-year-old has been brought before the court that morning. He is brief and to the point. It takes him just 65 words to make his case for detaining the three-year-old defendant in an industrial institution for 13 years.

> *"Teresa Mullaney, who appears to this court to be a child under the age of fifteen years (having been born as far as has been ascertained on the 9th June 1947) and who resides at Thurles in the County of Tipperary N.R., has been destitute not being an orphan and is illegitimate and her mother is unable to support her and consents to her committal."*

For its part, the court has no wish to dwell unduly on the matter either, declaring itself satisfied *"that it is expedient to deal with the said child by sending her to a certified industrial school."*

> *"It is hereby ordered,"* Justice Gleeson rules, *"that the said child shall be sent to the certified industrial school, the managers whereof are willing to receive her to be there detained until, but not including, the 9th day of June 1963."*

On that day, Tessie Mullaney will be exactly 16 years old and will have spent all of her childhood and half of her teenage years detained in an industrial institution.

It is unlikely that anyone in the courtroom expressed any concerns about what life might be like for a three-year-old girl shortly to be taken from their midst and detained in such an institution for the next 13 years of her life.

The business of the court was now almost done. Soon it would be time for lunch, and the topic of conversation for many in the courtroom was more likely to have been the exciting new plan that year by the local curate, Fr William Noonan, to set up a musical society in their town.

But if anyone had wondered about what lay ahead for the little girl, they would undoubtedly have been reassured when the court declared that the industrial school, run by the Sisters of Mercy, was *"conducted in accordance with the doctrines of the Catholic Church."*

But the court had not yet finished its business. Justice Gleeson had one more, very important item to attend to before lunch. He had to decide how much Mary Mullaney would be ordered to pay for her daughter's upkeep in the institution.

We are not sure how long the deliberations took or whether they were complicated by the fact that the court had already heard that, "her mother is unable to support her". In the event, the figure decided on was five shillings a week.

> *"It is further ordered,"* declared the judge, *"that Mary Mullaney residing at the County Home, Thurles, and parent of the said child shall pay to the Inspector of Reformatory and Industrial Schools a weekly sum of five shillings (5) until further order, the first payment to be made on the 1st day of August 1950."*

Since Tessie's sister had already been committed three years earlier, and her mother was paying five shillings for her, she now faced a hefty payment of 10 shillings per week for both daughters.

Within two months, Tessie's mother had begun to fall into arrears. The Department of Education Reformatory and Industrial Schools Branch alerted the Garda Superintendent in Thurles on 12 September 1950 as follows:

> *"With reference to the collector's report of the 9th instant, I am directed to ask for a report on the parent's present circumstances and ability to comply with the Court Order. It should be stated whether she is making a*

reasonable effort to pay or whether proceedings should be instituted for the recovery of arrears."

This was stamped received by the Superintendent's Office on 14 September and Sergeant McKenna was asked "for information and further attention". On 15 September, Sergeant McKenna asked Garda Kinsella "for further attention and report, please." Eight days later, on 23 September, Garda Laurence Kinsella wrote his report as follows:

"Parent Mary Mullaney is in poor circumstances. She paid one pound arrears on the 19th inst. She promises to pay off arrears when she gets employment."

Garda Kinsella's report is sent to the Inspector of reformatory and Industrial Schools where it is received on 26 September 1950.

Nine months pass and Mary Mullaney has moved from the County Home, where she had been living and working, and is now living with her elderly mother, who is very ill.

Her ailing mother needs constant care, so Mary cannot work. Payments have begun to fall behind again and she tries to seek a variation of the court order to "nil", writing the following letter to the Department of Education Reformatory and Industrial Schools Branch on 30 May 1951:

Kincora Tce
Thurles
Co. Tipp,

Dear Sir

I am writing to you on behalf of my child Teresa committed last July for which I am paying 5/- per week. I would be very grateful if you could reduce it to nil if possible, as my mother is an invalid. She is over 80 and she is not able to do anything for herself and I can't leave her and take up constant work.

Her letter is received by the Department on 31 May 1951. The Department takes immediate action and the investigative process is set in motion once again.

The Department writes to the Garda Superintendent in Thurles to investigate Mary Mullaney's ability to pay for her daughter. Attaching a copy of Mary Mullaney's letter, it says:

Department of Education,
Talbot House,
Talbot St.
Dublin

1 June 1951

Parental Money. Teresa Mullaney

"Please see attached communication from the parent in this case. A report on her ability to comply with the Court order is requested for the Inspector's information, please."

The letter is received by the Garda Superintendent in Thurles, on 2 June 1951 and once again, the Sergeant asks Garda Kinsella to call to Mary Mullaney to investigate.

One week later, on 9 June 1951, Garda Kinsella reports on the result of his latest investigation of Mary Mullaney.

Garda Síochána,
Thurles.

9.6.1951

To Sergt

Parental Money. Teresa Mullaney

"I beg to report that Mary Mullaney is now four weeks in arrears of parental money. She is at present residing with her mother who is an invalid. They are in poor circumstances financially. Owing to her mother's age and state of health, Mary is unable to take up employment, as she is the only person to look after her mother. In my opinion, she is unable to continue paying amount of 5/- in respect of her child Teresa.

Laurence Kinsella Garda 3802

Superintendent Convery sends Garda Kinsella's report to the Department, where it is received on 11 June 1951. Four days later, the Department inspector writes back to the Garda Síochána in Thurles, as follows:

Department of Education,
Reformatory and Industrial Schools Branch,
Talbot House,
Talbot Street,
Dublin.

15/6/51

Parental Money. Teresa Mullaney

"With reference to your minute of 11th inst of Collector's report I am directed to state that if you are satisfied the parent is unable to comply with the contribution order the Collector should advise payer to apply to the Court to have the order varied (reduced to "nil").

In this connection, I am to refer you to Sec. 75 Childrens Act 1908 as amended by Sec 22 Childrens Act 1941.

Please return these papers when further developments are being reported."

One month later, on 14 July1951, Mary Mullaney makes her application to the Court as follows:

Kincora Terrace
Thurles
Co Tipp

14. 7. 51

I am notifying you that I am putting an application before the Court at Thurles on first day of August 1951 in order to get the 5/- put on me for my child Teresa Mullaney varied.

Mary Mullaney

The District Court hears the application and its decision is recorded by Garda Kinsella and sent to the Department of Education.

Division of Tipperary
District Thurles.
Station Thurles.

2nd August 1951

Parental Money. Teresa Mullaney

At the Thurles District Court held on the 1st inst, Mary Mullaney parent of Teresa Mullaney made application to have Contribution Order made on 5.7.1950 reduced. Justice Gleeson after hearing evidence of Parent's circumstances reduced amount from 5/- to 2/6 to take effect from the 1.8.1951

Laurence Kinsella Garda 3802

By this time, Tessie Mullaney has been in the industrial school for over a year. But in the many reports and investigations that year of her mother's ability to comply with the court's contribution order, we find not a single reference in any of them to Tessie's welfare or even a passing comment from Department officials on how she might be faring generally.

But what we learn from her sister Mary, who was already in the institution on the afternoon that Tessie arrived after her court appearance, is profoundly shocking.

It is a picture of a terrified three-year-old little girl. She is screaming for her mother. She is bereft and inconsolable.

Unlike what happened in many other institutions, the nuns in this case told Tessie when she arrived that Mary was her sister. But since the sisters were like complete strangers to one another, this did nothing to calm the three year old.

"Mary told me I kicked the door screaming for my mother, kicking and screaming out for her. The nun said Mary was my sister and I started screaming at her too. My sister left me alone. She never bothered with me. I asked her years later, why, and she said 'because when I went near you, you screamed at me."

Tessie's first memory of the institution is of seeing girls scrubbing the yard. "Sr. A (name supplied) was there and a girl with a stick was hitting one of them across the back. I don't know what she had done."

Another terrifying early memory at the age of about four is of being locked in a broom cupboard to stop her crying.

"I remember being locked in a room under the stairs, you weren't allowed to cry. You were left there till you stopped crying. And to the day I left that orphanage, every time I passed that stairs, I got a creepy feeling.

"Sr. A had a leather belt that she used. There was always someone getting beaten. If it wasn't you, you were seeing it happen to someone else."

But however bad it was under Sr. A, it was "like torture" when she was away and the bigger girls were in charge.

Tessie vividly remembers two "really cruel weeks" when two bigger girls of about 15 were put in complete charge of the smaller girls while Sr. A was on holidays.

"When Sr. A went on holidays it was like torture. We were only five or six at that time and I remember to this day what they did.

"They wouldn't let us play. They wouldn't let us talk. They made us sit on benches all day. At night, it was worse. They'd put us to bed. They'd tuck us in. And then they'd go around at night and bang your pillow and if you blinked they'd pull you out of the bed and they'd beat you up with their hands. 'Twas a game with them. They did it every night for two weeks. I remember my brain nearly going. I was about six. Sometimes, the bigger girls were worse than the nuns.

"To be honest, when you got beaten they lost control. It wasn't just one slap. It was more a flogging you got. They'd been beaten black and blue themselves like that. It was like a cycle. That's what they'd seen and I probably would have done the same but I never got a chance to do the same, well thank God I didn't.

"When we were small the nuns used to take us out each morning, there was only one toilet for each dormitory. We, the younger ones, were in the Sacred Heart dormitory. They'd hit you with a shoehorn on the bare bottom if you wet the bed. And then you were sent to school with the sheet around your head."

Tessie escaped this humiliation because her mother, who had apparently heard about this practice, had made sure Tessie was trained not to wet the bed. "It never happened to me because my mother said she knew what went on and she trained me before I went there."

Tessie seems grateful for this, and not at all shocked or angry that her mother was aware of some of the secret suffering in the institution to which she had consented to commit her daughter.

"I don't think about it that way. I just thought that was how it was for me."

The cruelty was pervasive. Like being beaten into a bath of hot water.

"Miss B (name supplied) used to boil the water on the range and she'd put it into the baths. She used to beat us into the hot water in our nude. She'd have a stick and she'd be beating us and we'd be screaming. We didn't want to get into it; it was too hot.

"Miss B was the cook but Sr. A used to let her do a lot of jobs. Sr. A would do the same herself. Your legs would be red, your bottom would be red, you'd get beaten into it. Then you'd get your hair washed and they'd get a big jug of ice-cold water and pour it over your head".

Tessie shudders as she recalls another horrific incident.

"After we waxed the floors we'd tie rags on our feet and shine the floors that way. I loved it, sliding around the place, laughing. I was in third class and one day the nun teaching another class, Sr. B, came out and shouted 'Tess Mullaney come down here', and took me into her classroom.

"She closed the door. I don't remember coming out, she beat me up so much. Two girls had to bring me back to the orphanage. I know Sr. A was very upset over what happened because the nun from my class was complaining, asking what happened, I was black and blue from the big stick she belted me with."

But the mental suffering was almost worse. "They made you wait for the beating. I can take a beating; I'd rather be beaten. You'd be made stand facing the wall, without your dinner, and you'd go to bed without your dinner. Sr. A would do that. Or you'd have to stand and wait outside her office for a beating.

"The last beating I ever got, I remember it well. Sr. A had me in charge of the furnace. We were after having our tea and Sr. A asked me where I was going. I told her I was going down to the furnace. I was maybe 14 or

15. She said, 'Oh Tessie is a good girl' and I turned around and stuck out my tongue and went down to the furnace. When I came back, the girls said, 'she caught you, she caught you.'

"The girls started to kneel down to say the rosary and I started kneeling down and next thing she dashed into the room and beat me over the head, across the face and everywhere she could beat me. The girls were darting away to escape the stick. Then she started saying the rosary; she was still shaking.

"Another thing she did to me was terrible. Sr. A didn't like my spirit. But she never destroyed my spirit. We were having porridge this day and she said 'Tessie would like more and started scraping the pot and I ate it. Later on, she started the rosary but we'd no sooner started when I got very sick; I started vomiting. Two days later, we had an outing to Spanish Point (Co. Clare) but she wouldn't let me go. She said I was sick. I think she did it deliberately."

Tessie's mother visited her about twice a year but Tessie never spoke about her life in the institution and her mother never asked her what it was like.

She was in her 30s before she attempted to speak to her mother about what she had suffered.

"I said to her one day, I was well in my 30s, and d'you know, she didn't want to talk about it. I said 'you don't know what we put up with in the orphanage.' She said 'of course I do'. And I said 'do you know they put sheets on the girls' heads when they were going to school?' She said 'I knew about all that. That's why I had you well trained before you went.' There was a woman in the orphanage who came out. I think that's how she knew.

"To be honest, and I think about it a lot, I never got to talk to her. I never knew what to say to her. My mother was ashamed of herself all her life because she had us. She was literally ashamed of herself. She never liked to be called 'Mammy'.

"She told me when she had me baptised and was bringing me up to the cathedral in Thurles people walked on the other side of road rather than walk with her."

She also told Tessie that she had been thrown out of the church one morning.

"She was full of guilt. She used to say 'God will never forgive me for having you.'

When Tessie's mother visited her at the institution, she'd bring her bananas and fig rolls and the nuns gave her mother "high tea of sandwiches and buns". Sr. A used to come and sit down and talk to her; they both came from the same village. They'd talk about this person and that person."

Her mother also sent Tessie presents, which Tessie still remembers fondly. "She bought me a lovely jumper one time; I still remember the jumper and skirt. But the skirt was too small and the nuns gave it to another girl, I was about 11 or 12. The jumper was purple and had a sailor's collar. The skirt was red."

As Tessie got older, the violence in the institution began to lessen. It was the 1960s now and the nuns began to take in fewer "orphans" and began taking in fee-paying boarders instead.

"They took over four of our dormitories, so there was only one dormitory of us left. And we did all the work for them. We were kept off from school. We had to wash their bras by hand, their shirts and socks and knickers by hand.

"Every Saturday I used to go around and collect all the sanitary towels and light a fire in the range and burn all the sanitary towels. I had to fill the furnace twice a day with a wheelbarrow of anthracite. When you opened it up, all the soot would come out and cover you, and the fumes would get up your nose. In the summer I was put inside it to clean it with rags."

Tessie remembers how she suffered on another occasion at the hands of the cook.

"I had to collect six buckets of potatoes and go to the trough and scrub them and leave them at the back door for next day's dinner. One day the cook called me in and asked me to whip cream and she said 'I'll tell you when to stop'.

"So I whipped and whipped and whipped it into butter. Then she said 'look what you're after doing' and she gave me a big bash across the head. Then she went over to the press and she brought out a big pot, and she got a fistful of salt and she mixed it and she said, 'you'll eat that up every day till it's gone', and I had to. Every day, she spread it on two slices of bread. All that salt. It went on for a week or two.

"My sister worked in the kitchen and she said something happened one day and the cook grabbed her by the head of the hair and dragged her and kicked her in the ribs.

"A lot of this went on behind Sr. A's back. I don't know if she knew it was going on, but nothing was done about it. She never asked when we were black and blue. The girls were given free rein."

Tessie's sister came back to visit the institution after she left, but not to see Tessie. "She'd be visiting her friends. And Sr. A had her pet and Mary would bring her out for the day and she bought her things but nothing for me. She bought her a doll. I tore the head off that doll, I was so jealous."

"My mother told me later my sister blamed me for her being in the orphanage because she was taken to the orphanage after I was born." When she asked her sister about this, Mary told her "you just kicked and screamed, so I stayed away from you."

But Tessie Mullaney was neither excited nor happy when on 8 June 1963, one day before her 16th birthday, as had been stipulated by the court in Thurles 13 years earlier, she was "released on supervision" from the industrial school.

Her "Notice of Discharge" said she was being sent as a "general servant to Sisters of Mercy, Lourdes Hospital (Rochestown Avenue, Dun Laoghaire, later known as the National Rehabilitation Hospital). Her wages were £2 a week.

The notice also stated that, "a supervision certificate has been issued and the health authority notified".

The notice was sent to the Inspector Reformatory and Industrial Schools Branch, who sent a copy to the Superintendent, Garda Síochána, Thurles, seeking to resolve the issue of "parental moneys". In this copy, "released on supervision" becomes "discharged". The Inspector's memo to the superintendent with the Notice of Discharge on 8 June 1963 read:

> *"The above particulars are for the information of the Collector of Parental Moneys. The Parent is liable to contribute for the period his child was in the school and to pay up arrears, if any. In case of revocation of licence, the contribution re-commences from the date of re-admission to the School.*

Kindly report below if any arrears are outstanding, and if it is expected
that they will be collected in due course. If you do not expect that the arrears
will be collected, do you recommend (a) prosecution of the parent or (b)
remission of the arrears (reasons for either recommendation to be given)?

T Mac Diabhid, Cigire"

This is received by the Garda Síochána in Thurles and on 20 June 1963.
The "Inspector for the Supt" asks Sgt McKenna to alert "Collector
Garda McCormack who will report in accordance with A overleaf". On
3 July, Garda McCormack completes his report as follows:

"Arrears outstanding on the 8.6.63 £78.11.6. I do not expect to collect
them. I would recommend remission of the arrears as the child's mother is in
Co Home at Thurles in very poor circumstances."

On 5 July 1963, Superintendent J Ryan sent the report to the Inspector,
Industrial and Reform Schools, Dublin, as follows:

Please see the report overleaf. In the circumstances, I recommend remission
of the arrears due.

Tessie Mullaney had now begun work as a "general servant" at the
Lourdes Hospital in Dun Laoghaire, where her sister Mary was also
working. "I got a job there in the convent kitchen. They sent me to work
in the wards giving out the food. They asked me one day if I'd feed one
particular patient. I fed the lady and after that, she didn't want anyone to
feed her except me. One day I was sent for and the nuns asked me if I
wanted to be a nurse. They said they'd train me."

Tessie thought she would probably like to be a nurse but in the end, she
believed dreams like that were for other people.

"I said no. I think I would have liked it but I didn't have the confidence
for it then. I never had any confidence. They told you in the orphanage
you were no good, you were useless.

"I wasn't able to read properly either. I could learn things off by heart
but not read well. It was because I needed glasses, but all those years I
didn't have them."

But the old fears still haunted her at the hospital. Since it was run by the Sisters of Mercy, it felt to Tessie like she was being detained again. She soon left and began drifting from job to job, with little education and little understanding of the facts of life.

Tessie was now 17 and just a year out of the institution. Her life was about to change again. Soon, totally unprepared, Tessie Mullaney would become pregnant. She describes how casually it happened, her raw innocence at the time.

"We were locked in at night at the hospital. They didn't pay us – we just got a few bob if we needed it. A girl with me wanted to go up the road to the shop. These two motorbikes came flying down the road and she went 'yooooh' at the fellas, and they stopped and started talking. I didn't say two words. But they were nice. They gave us a spin on the motorbikes. Then I ended up pregnant, not my friend."

"We left the hospital. We didn't like it there. I still didn't know I was pregnant. I think we got a few shillings from the nuns. We went to Loughlinstown Hospital and we got jobs there.

"They wanted us to start straight away but we wanted to take a few days off first so we told them we were still working in the other place. The next week we went to the job and the nun said, 'I will not take liars in here.' So we left."

Tessie, now pregnant, was also homeless.

"The other girl knew someone who had a flat and we moved in with her, but we had no money. I was getting sicker and sicker and I was three weeks with nothing to eat. The landlord was shouting for his rent. I got very run down.

"My sister met me and she said I should come back to the hospital in Dun Laoghaire. So next thing I was back working there and one day one of the girls called and said the doctor wanted to see me.

"The doctor said I was pregnant. I wasn't that surprised at that stage because of how I'd been feeling. I stayed on working there up until a month before the baby was born. Then the nuns told me about the Mother and Baby Home on the Navan Road in Dublin."

"When I was pregnant I used to have dreams that they'd screw off the head and arms so the baby could get out. No-one ever told me anything."

And thus in the Mother and Baby home, with loneliness and dread as her companions, the young mother gave birth to a healthy boy.

Whether she wanted to keep her son or not would never arise. "They made you sign papers. I didn't know what I was signing. You signed your baby away. To be honest, I suppose I thought that was the way it was. Like what my mother did. I signed him away before he was born. That was the system, I thought. That was the way it was.

"I was very innocent. I remember being upset. I used to go in and out to visit him. One time I brought him a little yellow suit. It was for his adoption. He was adopted at six months.

"I was in the institution at three but I was never angry at my mother for what she did; I never blamed her. She had to put Mary in the orphanage when she had me. Mary is very bitter about that. She left to make a place for me, they wouldn't have two there. That's what they did in the County Home, there were a few other kids like me there and the mothers worked there. I know my mother hated it there. She ran away a few times, but the guards brought her back."

Tessie shows a picture of her mother with five women from the County Home. "All the five women had babies, all went into the County Home and the babies were sent to the institutions, I think that's how they worked it."

A number of the girls with Tessie in the institution were from the Thurles area, and when their mothers visited, they would visit Tessie too. "Their mothers spent all their lives in the County Home doing kitchen work and laundry work and patient work until they died."

After leaving the Mother and Baby home Tessie got a cleaning job with a couple in Terenure in Dublin, but she didn't like it. "The woman took in lodgers and I was cleaning till 11 at night. She was hard. Once I called her a bitch under my breath but her sister heard me. They told me to get out. But where was I to go. So I went back to the Mother and Baby Home on the Navan Road and they took me in and I worked there for a while."

More casual jobs followed but as Tessie approached 21, she found what was probably the nearest thing to a home. "It was with a couple on the Navan Road looking after their two adopted kids. I had my 21st birthday there; she gave me a party.

"The only people I had as friends all my life were the girls from the orphanages; they were the only ones I trusted. My friends said we'd go to Dalkey Island, so we got a boat. That's where I spent my 21st birthday. We sat on Dalkey Island for the day and when we came back, she had a party for me. Her husband was a vet. They were very nice. I worked there for three years."

Over the years, Tessie wondered about her son, though she kept in touch with his father. "Danny was his name. We stayed in touch. I met him a few times." They decided to get engaged. But when Tessie went to England to work with a family for a year, Danny stayed behind in Dublin.

"While I was in England he started going with another girl. So when I came back I broke it off with him. I went to the church in Foxrock, said a few prayers and then I came out and he was waiting and I gave him the ring and said goodbye.

"He said what are you going to do now and I said I'm going to meet a tall, dark, handsome man and get married. And I did. We lived together for two years first and then we got married. I was 24."

Then, one morning, 26 years later, Tessie's son came back into her life. "I was shocked at first. The nuns in the institution rang me to say he was looking for me."

Tessie had told her husband but not their five children about her son. "I'm a very open person and when something happens I face it. I explained to them what had happened.

"He came and met me and stayed for two nights. He showed me a baby picture of himself. In it, he had the suit I'd bought him. He turned out lovely, a gorgeous man. He'd done very well for himself, a businessman in Galway."

Soon after she had met her son, another shock awaited her. Tessie and her husband had been married for 27 years "but one day he just walked out of the marriage. He had another woman."

Tessie's life was in turmoil, haunted now by sorrow as well as fear.

"I'd blocked out everything until I saw *Dear Daughter* (RTÉ documentary in 1996 about Goldenbridge). It hit me really badly for the first time. I cried for nearly three days.

"I realised I was always on edge, with my kids especially, in case anything would happen and I always had to have the house spick and span, even with five kids. It was the fear from the orphanage that someone would come and see it dirty. I always had that fear.

"My children didn't understand either at first how absolutely terrible the orphanage was. You weren't allowed to be a child, and my children didn't understand because I only told them about the devilment I got up to. Like the time I threw potatoes at one girl and by the time we were finished, the place was mess. I also ran a trolley at her. I told them about things like that, but not the bad things, the beatings afterwards.

"There used to be times I used to feel so down, not depressed, as down. There was a fear with you and to this day, I have that fear.

"The orphanage was terrible, absolutely terrible. But I wasn't bitter. I'm not a bitter person. And that's why you think it mightn't be affecting me because I don't have bitterness about things. But the orphanage was absolutely terrible."

Mary is in England now and married with children but the two sisters have little contact.

Tessie keeps in touch with her half-sister, Philomena, who was born a few years after Tessie. Philomena had contracted TB as a child but that also saved her from the institution. Her mother raised her for a few years and then she was fostered with a local family.

Tessie's mother, her grandmother and her uncle had been living in the same house in Thurles, but after Tessie was born her uncle Jack, who was in the Irish army, left and went to England.

Soon afterwards, when Tessie's mother was in danger of losing the house, she asked Jack, who owned it, to come home to help.

"But Jack never came home and she lost the house. Her family disowned her. She stayed in the County Home then until she died."

And on the day her mother lay dying, two months short of her 83rd birthday, in the County Home in Thurles in February 1991 Philomena and Tessie were at her bedside. It was Tessie who was holding her mother's hand when she died.

Some of Mary Mullaney's secrets would now die with her. But others were about to be revealed and they would shock her daughter.

"You'll get a shock when I die," her mother had told Tessie a few weeks earlier. She had asked Tessie to get a suitcase she'd put in another room in the County Home. But Tessie was afraid if she started looking for the case, she might be stopped "I had no confidence in myself then, none at all, the fear of authority. I couldn't get it."

Tessie remains convinced that the suitcase must have held clues, secrets about her mother's life and her own and she regrets to this day not retrieving it from the room in the County Home before her mother died.

She never saw the suitcase until after the funeral. And by then it was too late. Any secrets it had held had been destroyed.

On the day her mother died, Tessie learned later in Thurles, a local man working in the County Home had been asked to burn everything in the suitcase. Documents were burned, photos destroyed, letters lost forever.

"I don't know why they were burned. I was very hurt over that. I never got over it. I could have learned a lot. She was a very proud person, and very secretive. I might have learned about the family."

But it's hard to keep some secrets in an Irish town.

"The day after my mother died the nurse asked 'is your brother coming to the funeral?' I said 'I don't have a brother'. She said, 'that's funny because I met an old lady down the town and she said Mary Mullaney had three boys and three girls.' Philomena, who had already heard a rumour about a brother, said 'I told you, I told you.'

"To be honest with you, we couldn't even mourn her after that, we were thinking so much, so worried about these other brothers. We thought we might have one. I remember my mother told me he died when he was a little boy, but nothing else, she was vague about him. Now we had three. It was a shock.

"I have a photo of my mother and she has her hand on the shoulder of a little boy. We went looking for him, he was John, and we found out we had two others."

The story about her brothers was confirmed again when Tessie visited her mother's friend at the time of the funeral.

"My mother's friend had moved to Borrisoleigh and I went to see her after the funeral and I asked her if my mother had any boys. She was very firm about it. 'She had three,' she said, 'John, Jamie and Patrick. Your mother loved her kids, loved every one of you, and she'd never have given any of you away, never.'

"She said my mother's family were all big farmers. Maybe the boys moved in with them. I don't know. I also know my grandmother had an uncle, named Joyce. He'd had an electrical shop in Dublin and after 1916, he sold up and went to America. He came over twice a year from America. Maybe he took them to America, I don't know. I'm not sure I'd want to know them now, it's too late."

Tessie also discovered she had cousins who were priests. "At her funeral, there were seven priests on the altar." Five of the priests, she found out, were her mother's cousins.

"I've never seen such a big funeral in all my life. There were cousins there that didn't know we existed. I'd learned the night before the funeral that this fellow and that fellow were my cousins. After the funeral we went to this big house, he was another cousin of mine whose kids went to Trinity College. They were all my cousins."

Did she feel angry about that? "No, maybe there's something wrong with me," Tessie smiles. "I was told we might even have had a bishop in the family on my grandmother's side. My mother was full of secrets. She used to go to weddings and jubilees of cousins and I said to her one time why don't you introduce us, but she wouldn't."

Tessie was more upset later than shocked when she discovered her cousins. "I was more upset with my mother. She'd kept us away from our family. She used to say to me when I visited her 'my cousin was in today', and I'd say 'why don't you introduce us' and she'd say 'they don't want anything to do with you. They wouldn't want to know you.'"

Her mother was right, it seems. When Tessie went to Thurles for the month's mind, four weeks after her mother's death, she was told: "You don't have to come down here anymore; we'll look after her grave."

Tessie ignored them, "I went down anyway." It was the kind of defiance her mother would probably have liked, because once she too had been defiant.

During the years when Tessie's mother was a young girl, Tipperary had become a flashpoint in the War of Independence. When Mary Mullaney was 12, in March 1920, the Black and Tans were sent to Ireland and began a reign of terror, particularly in Tipperary, Limerick and Cork.

That year, in reprisal attacks, the 'Tans burned and sacked a number of villages and towns, including Balbriggan in Dublin and Templemore and Thurles in Tipperary. By the end of the year, martial law had been enforced across Tipperary, Limerick, Kerry and Cork. Sean Tracey and

Dan Breen had become local legends but the women of Tipperary, including Tessie's grandmother, played a major role too in the ranks of Cumann na mBan.

Tessie's grandmother was a key figure in the local campaign, acting as a spy for the IRA and passing on information she had gathered while working as a cook for the English soldiers.

Tessie recalls that her own mother played a crucial role as a "runner" to the IRA with the information from Tessie's grandmother.

Mary Mullaney later joined Cumann na mBan and Tessie proudly displays her membership badge as she recounts her mother's exploits. "When my mother visited us in Dublin – she'd often come up for holidays for two or three months – she'd tell the grandchildren about Cumann na mBan and march around the kitchen for them, laughing, with a pretend wooden gun.

"My grandmother was acting as a spy for the IRA while working as a cook for the English soldiers. When she was cooking for them she'd hear some of the conversations, she'd pick up bits of information. She'd tell my mother and my mother would run across the fields to the IRA men. My mother told me that when she was about 12 two soldiers were killed after some information was passed on. She felt guilty about that. She said if she hadn't passed on the information they wouldn't have been killed."

The historical records of IRA actions in Tipperary during 1920 attest to a number of ambushes or killings of soldiers and RIC in the Thurles area.

We will never know whether the information passed on by Tessie's mother and grandmother contributed to these actions during the War of Independence in Tipperary, but when her mother died Tessie learned that she should have had a military funeral.

"We got a letter from the Cumann na mBan afterwards. They said she should have got a military funeral but they didn't get word in time that she'd died. They came to the month's mind and apologised. I would have liked that, she probably would too."

The son of a good friend of her mother's in Thurles told Tessie he knew who her father was. Her father had emigrated to England, the man told her. But he was dead now, he said.

Tessie will probably never know the full truth. But she did find one photograph, carefully hidden under the lining of her mother's suitcase in the County Home after she died.

"It was underneath brown paper. I don't know who he is. My mother used to go to that case. She'd always go to that case for a few bob if you were down to see her."

It is a photograph of a very handsome man and the likeness to him on the features of Tessie Mullaney's face is striking. But her mother has written nothing on the back, no clue as to why the photograph was important or why she had kept it over all the years.

"You dream, but I don't know. He could be my father, or he could be someone else's. The photo and a pair of brown leather boots. That was all I found. That was all that was left. It leaves you in wonderland. It was mean of her to do that, to leave us in wonderland. Sure, she didn't even tell us about the boys. I'm not a bitter-minded person. Maybe I'm an eejit to be that way."

Tessie recently found her brother John's death certificate. "He died like she'd said as a little boy. She wasn't lying after all. I felt good about that."

Like most of the children who passed through these industrial institutions, Tessie Mullaney has suffered the loss not only of her childhood but of her adulthood too. The suffering in childhood continued to haunt and blight her adult years, the fear, the lack of trust, the loss of love and lasting relationships, pain hidden, shame concealed, families unaware of each other's existence, questions unanswered, whispers of truths or half-truths, and always the pain that never ceases.

"There's hurt always inside. We (survivors) go into ourselves. We never learned to stand up for ourselves. I often walked the road and all of a sudden, this sense of loneliness would come into you, deep down. I get that often, especially that sense of loneliness, emptiness.

"I suppose I survived because of my spirit. They never broke that."

Today Tessie Mullaney's spirit is reflected in an art form that has endured for over a thousand years. A pink stained glass butterfly stands out from among the objects she has crafted since she began working with glass over a decade ago.

"I was interested in art and it was my daughter who suggested stained glass. I started in September 2000. I was very nervous; it took a long time for me to get the hang of it. I persevered. It took two or three years.

"Art is my salvation."

9

STORY OF CARMEL MCDONNELL-BYRNE

"I remember the horror of hearing my brothers had died in care
but I wasn't allowed to grieve"

Carmel McDonnell-Byrne betrays none of the pain that has convulsed her life. She is poised and elegant with a quick smile. It is at night the anguish emerges.

It is then she relives the terror of hearing her brothers had died accidentally while in an institution. Or it can be a simple thing, like having a glass of water at her bedside that will trigger nightmares of bed-wettings, beatings and the screams of children.

There are other nightmares too. One nightmare appears like a scene from a concentration camp. A little girl is stealing food for her baby brother, who is tugging at her. She knows how hungry he is. She thinks there is no food anywhere. She is frightened but desperate. Somehow, she finds her way to the pantry and is shocked by what she sees.

The pantry is stocked to capacity: Long tins of corned beef, large catering pans of bread, large tins of jams, tins of biscuits, boxes of cheese, cocoa powder, barley soup mix with red lentils, large jars of Bovril, large bags of porridge, eggs, tall jars of sweets, many packets of Birds angels delight, large tins of Birds custards, many packets of corn flour, packets of semolina and tapioca, large packets of loose tea. Mostly, items she's never seen before, stored there for the teachers.

She wonders what she can steal that won't be noticed. There are so many different varieties of jelly. She decides on one packet and moves the others around so it won't be noticed. She is starving too but she doesn't take any of the jelly for herself. She believes that God will punish her if she does.

"My little brother was always so hungry. I used to carry him on my hip to take him into the recreation room every morning before anyone else got there. I showed him how to pick up the cod-liver oil tablets that children had spat out the previous day when the staff weren't looking. They were difficult to pick up when the oil had emptied out, so the secret was to wet your finger and the shells would hold to your finger like glue."

Carmel is reliving exactly what happened at Goldenbridge Industrial School in Dublin, run by the Sisters of Mercy in the relatively progressive Ireland of the late Sixties when Carmel was 10 and her brother was just two.

On other nights, in another nightmare, Carmel is terrified by piercing laughter. Here, again, she is reliving the chilling detail of what actually happened in Goldenbridge.

The piercing laughter tonight is coming from an older girl who is looking after Carmel's two-year-old brother and another brother who is three. Carmel has seen this girl beating her baby brothers before but on this night, the girl is not beating them. Instead, she is walking quietly with them.

They are moving towards a wall. Then the girl stops and reaches down for their hands. It is then the piercing laughter starts.

She takes their baby fingers and sticks them into an electric socket, holding them there until Carmel's brothers reel in shock. Then the laughter gets louder. "She thought this was so funny. Of course she did it to other children too," Carmel shudders at the memory. "This girl had been brutalised and she brutalised others. That's what happened in Goldenbridge."

It was to Goldenbridge that Carmel and her five brothers and two sisters had been taken by her father one month after her mother walked out of the family home. It was August 1965, the month that Carmel turned 10.

"My mother left on the 9th of July 1965 during the summer holidays. Both of my parents had been out; we didn't know where they were. When they returned my mother started packing. She told all of us to go to the field near our house, all of us except my eldest brother. He was 14. We didn't stay out too long. We were kind of suspicious, so we sneaked back in.

"My mother was gone. My father was there. My uncle was there too. I overheard a conversation between my father and my uncle and court was mentioned. Looking back now, it might have been a barring order she tried to get against my father. Up to that point, she couldn't live with him nor could she live without him. In good times, he used to buy her LPs. There was always music in our house. Then there was the other side. She had eight of us and there were numerous miscarriages."

Carmel still hoped her mother would return, just like she had so many times before. "She was often sick or in hospital having one of us. She had a heart problem so had to be hospitalised for most of the pregnancy and then she'd come home.

"I was in and out of Madonna Home from the age of 15 months. But each time, I returned home to my Mammy and Daddy. Then, from the age of four, I was placed in St. Anne's Industrial School in Booterstown (Dublin). The times I spent there were sporadic. My earliest memories are of acute hunger and feeling extremely cold. I wet my bed regularly, despite the inevitable beating that followed.

"Although my sister was with me in St. Anne's, it made little difference because every time we were caught talking to each other we were beaten. This was because we were supposed to sit silently with our fingers on our lips during the day. I remember those nuns so well. To me they seemed like huge monsters at the time. I constantly longed to be at home with my Mammy and Daddy and my other siblings."

Carmel and her sister did return home again from St. Anne's when their mother came out of hospital following the birth of another child. At about the age of five, Carmel remembers learning an unusual skill from her mother – how to make rosary beads. "Perhaps she had been in an institution herself as a child. She also taught me how to knit and I knitted my first Aran sweater before I went to Goldenbridge."

Carmel had become accustomed to this cycle now: first the painful separations, then the joyful reunions. But this cycle ended in the summer of 1965.

"When my mother left that July it was decided we would stay with relatives but that didn't work out. My father said he didn't want to split us up, that we'd all go to the one place. He was a hospital porter and did labouring jobs as well. But by August, with all eight of us at home during the summer holidays, he wasn't managing very well."

She doesn't know if he had planned it like this, but it was exactly two days before her 10th birthday that her father set out with Carmel and her two sisters and five brothers, on August 28, 1965, on a journey that was to shatter their lives.

None of them had any inkling of what lay ahead as they left their home in Dublin that bright summer morning. Indeed the eight of them, ranging in age from two to 14 years, must have cut quite a happy family picture to anyone who saw them walking beside their father in the August sunshine.

The children even felt a ripple of excitement as they listened to their father. Carmel's birthday was approaching and he'd begun talking about a party.

"My father told us we were going to a party. Everyone had their Sunday best on. I remember we were walking farther and farther from our house. I kept looking back. I could still see it for a long time. Then my home disappeared.

"We walked up this long avenue and there was this large building ahead. It sent a shiver down my spine. It reminded me of St. Anne's. I remember we went into this office and there were all these papers that my father signed. I was in a state of shock. The two older boys (aged 11 and 12) were too old for Goldenbridge so they left with my father, along with my older brother. I learnt later they went to St Saviour's in Dominic Street (Dublin). The eldest boy, who was 14, returned home with my father as he was of working age. There were no hugs or goodbyes.

"We were marched down to the recreation room. It seemed like hundreds of children were seated on the wooden benches on three sides of the recreation room, with fingers on their lips. I was terrified. All I wanted to do was go home. Our own clothes were taken from us. Our hairs were cut above the ears.

"The following week my father visited and he was very angry about the state of our hair. He said he'd speak to the nuns about it. We were constantly afraid. We knew we weren't in a nice place but I couldn't talk to him about it, we were afraid to say anything, to ask any questions. There was always a lay teacher present in the visiting room. We were given a number. Mine was 113. It appeared to me that Harry and Robert were freer in St Saviour's than we were and sometimes they accompanied my father on visits to us."

Carmel now became the eldest of her family in Goldenbridge. Along with her were her two baby brothers and her two younger sisters. "I automatically took on the role of looking after the others. Any chance I got I looked out for food for them.

"At teatime the non-bedwetters got two slices of bread and a cup of cocoa. The slices were piled on top of one another and if you delayed, either because of a punishment or a chore, another child robbed your ration. You didn't tell on anyone because they would get you back."

And if you happened to get sick at mealtime, you were brutally humiliated. "Every time we were given pink luncheon roll I used to throw up on my plate and the staff would force me to eat everything from my plate, including the vomit. I feel physically sick every time I have to recall those memories."

The Sacred Heart dormitory in Goldenbridge was known as "the-wet-the-bed-dormitory". The lay teachers slept in cubicles and supervised the dormitories. Carmel slept in a section that was closest to the staff cubicles. "I was terrified of sleeping so close to people who terrified me. I didn't know the minute they'd come out of their cubicle and pounce on me for going to the toilet. I couldn't go to the toilet whenever I felt like it, I had to sneak out and I was always worried in case they caught me. There were set times when we went to the toilet but because we were all so traumatised many of the children, including myself, wet the bed.

"One of the lay staff caught me many a night as I tried to sneak to the toilet. She would thump me very hard anywhere and order me back to bed. Inevitably, I still managed to soak the bed. I was so scared of the punishment. I had to take my wet sheet off the bed and bring it to the head nun for examination. Like the other children, I had to line up for a beating.

"It didn't really matter whether you were first or last, the punishment was still horrific. Sometimes I thought that being last was the worst for me. I remember one time when I was last. I was feeling so frightened and anxious, wishing I was at home with my mammy, daddy and all of my brothers and sisters. I was told to turn my knuckles upwards towards the ceiling. The nun gave me six of the hardest slaps on each bare knuckle, with a wooden hand brush. My hands and fingers were stinging.

"After the beating I had to make my daily quota of rosary beads. It was excruciating and took me longer than normal to finish. I also had to wash the sheet in the cold washroom and then put it in the dryer so I could reuse the sheet that night. All bedwetters were deprived of water from midday. You can imagine how thirsty we were. We often had to resort to drinking from the toilet bowl – it didn't matter whether it was dirty, we were so thirsty and needed to quench our thirst.

"Although I know this bed-wetting punishment will never happen to me again, to this day I still wake up many times during the night scared of wetting my bed. Going to bed for me is still a very traumatic experience when it should be a place of peace. I am still haunted by it. But, as I slowly adapt, I am learning to allow myself to have as much water by my bedside as I please."

But all the pain, all the trauma, the constant hunger, the humiliation, the wanton cruelty, the absence of any measure of human warmth, all these were nothing compared to the horror that awaited Carmel on July 10, 1966, one year after she had arrived in Goldenbridge.

"On that Sunday I was called with my sister to the head nun's office. I wondered what crime I had committed and I was petrified waiting for her to open her office door. When I went into the office, I was surprised to see my uncle there. Instinctively, I knew by his expression that something dreadful had happened.

"He told us he had very bad news: that Harry and Robert and one of their friends had drowned the previous evening. They were on holiday in Donegal along with the other boys from St Saviour's in Dominic Street. My lovely brothers. It was too hard to understand, to grasp. I was in shock but I didn't cry, not then, you tried not cry in Goldenbridge. The nun told us to say our prayers and gave us two bull's eyes (sweets) each. I felt then and I still do today that she gave me a sweet for the life of each brother.

"I was very frightened. Now our family was getting smaller. This really frightened me. Harry and Robert died exactly a year to the day that our mother vanished. In the space of a year, we had lost our mother and our two brothers. I thought I was losing everything.

"Later that day I was scrubbing the long corridor on my hands and knees when I couldn't hold back the tears any longer. The realisation that I'd never see my brothers again hit me to the very core. One of the lay staff, noticed me crying. To my horror she slapped me across the face and told me to stop the silly nonsense. 'Sure haven't you other brothers and sisters,' she barked.

"That remark and the head nun's callousness haunted me for years and I was unable to let my brothers go. I wasn't allowed to grieve. I still go to bed with a copy of their memorial card under my pillow. I feel it's the only way I can protect them."

Forty-eight years have passed since Carmel's brothers died so suddenly and so tragically. Each day since Carmel still clings to the memory of the last time they met.

"They came to visit us from St Saviour's in Dominic St. It was quite early in the morning and they brought a lovely sponge cake with them. We sat near the statue of Our Blessed Lady. It was a particularly enjoyable time with them. Little did we know that it would be our last day with our beautiful brothers.

"My brothers arrived at Rossnowlagh that evening. They were allowed to swim at about seven o'clock. That's when our brothers and another boy died."

Carmel is still shattered by the loss of her beloved brothers. But years of counselling have helped her grieving process. It has been helped too by the compassion of a retired garda sergeant and his family in Donegal. Carmel met him in 1999 in response to an appeal she had made on local radio (Highland Radio) for information about her brothers' deaths. The retired garda sergeant told her that 33 years earlier, he had helped in the search for the missing boys.

"Everyone for miles around pitched in to help in the search for the bodies, and it had an enormous impact on the gardaí and the local people," he told Carmel. He said the other boys were found first and that he was on his own when he found Robert's body. His words helped to bring Carmel some solace. "Knowing that our brothers were treated with respect and dignity at the time of their deaths helped the healing process."

But back in Goldenbridge in 1966, the horror of her brothers' drowning haunted Carmel. She began to fear bath time in the institution because it brought flashbacks of their deaths.

"We were lined up in groups of four to six and we had to bathe together in the same bath. The water was filthy, with scum around the edges and was freezing cold. I just wanted to get out as quickly as possible, but a lay member of the staff wouldn't allow me out because she knew I was scared. She kept my head under the water until I would turn blue with the cold and gasping for air. I often thought how panicky my brothers must have felt when they realised that they were drowning and that there was no one there to save them. Even now, every time I step into a bath my brothers' last moments haunt me."

Carmel's other two younger brothers had now been in the institution for a year-and-a-half and were not faring well. She feared for their health and began to plead with her father to take them out.

"One day when my daddy visited I pleaded with him to take them home. One of them had repeated ear infections, requiring hospitalisation several times and my other brother was losing weight rapidly, and he too had been hospitalised because of his emaciated state."

Eventually, in March 1968, her father agreed to take them from Goldenbridge and he sent them to live with relatives in Birmingham. "My dad explained the relatives would love to take all of us but they didn't have the room."

Carmel never heard from her brothers again until 1972 when one of them arrived to Goldenbridge looking for his sisters. "It was a very tense reunion. We were like strangers. I had just completed my last exam for the Intermediate Certificate and was very stressed that I'd fail the exam and I didn't know what would become of me. I wondered if I'd be allowed leave Goldenbridge or would I continue to be abused there for many more years.

"Our family was growing smaller and smaller, now that my father and my older brother had moved to Manchester and the younger boys in Birmingham. That left just three of us trying to survive in Goldenbridge. I thought about my family every single day and I longed for news of how the younger boys were coping. I worried constantly about my mammy. Was she safe? When was she going to come and bring us home to our own house, were we could all be happy again?"

One particular day in the spring of 1967, when Carmel had turned 11½, she needed her mother more than ever in her life before. But her mother wasn't there and there was no one else there either to gently explain the facts of life to her. Instead, when Carmel saw she was losing blood she was seized with terror that she might be dying.

"One day my pants were wet. When I checked, I noticed blood. I thought I was dying. I wondered who would look after the rest of my family. On my way to the yard toilets, I found a piece of newspaper on the ground. I used it as a pad, to try and stop the blood before someone noticed. I arrived at the toilets. I washed my pants in the bowl in the freezing cold water. It was very difficult because I had no soap. I was also scared of being caught.

"Then I walked over to the outside vent that was for the tumble dryer and held my pants up to dry. It seemed to take forever and I became even more anxious trying to think what I would say if I was caught. I definitely knew I would be in trouble. That terrified me more than the fear of dying.

"I heard footsteps so I started to shake. Panic set in. I closed my eyes tightly, and when I opened them and looked across. It was one of the nice girls. When I told her about the blood, she just smiled and explained to me what was happening. She said that I should go to the medicine cabinet at a set time every day while I was bleeding and I'd get a clean pad. The problem was that I had so many chores to do that I was always missing the opening hours of the sanitary towel distribution and that meant that I had to wash the pad and reuse it over and over again." No allowance was made during girl's periods. Rather, it seemed to serve as an occasion for inflicting more humiliation.

"Each week boys and girls were lined up for a shower. It was absolutely freezing in the shower room. Some weeks we were treated for scabies with a white lotion called Benzyl Benzoate. It was painted onto our bodies. We only knew it as the itch stuff. It had a pungent smell and it caused burning to the skin and to the eyes. I only got the medical name of this solution some years ago and the instructions state 'not to be used on children unless diluted.' To the best of my knowledge, it was never diluted in Goldenbridge.

"On one particular occasion, when I had a period, I recall feeling so ashamed and humiliated having to expose my body in front of boys, let alone the girls, for that treatment. I found it impossible to relax because of the boys' presence. I never really understood why the head nun insisted on this exposure given that she was always calling the girls "man mad". She used this name calling even when I was carrying my own brother.

"We were literally painted with a wide emulsion paintbrush. We had to stand with our legs spread wide apart and our arms outstretched. My skin felt as though it was on fire. My eyes burnt and tears ran down my face. When it came to my turn for the treatment, she would hit me on the bare arms or slap me around the face. 'Now that will give you something to cry about,' she'd say. I believe she definitely got some sort of sexual gratification from this public exhibition. I have absolutely no doubt about it."

The humiliation and embarrassment had lasting effects on Carmel right into adulthood and blighted her relationship. "This forced nakedness caused huge problems in my marriage. I wouldn't undress in front of my husband, for fear of ridicule, in the same way the nun ridiculed me in the past. To this day, I still have problems undressing on a beach or in a public area. I am brought back to those horrendous days in Goldenbridge and I get panicky again."

Carmel kept on hoping that one day, her mother would finally come back and take them all home. She remembers a particular day when she longed desperately for her mother. "It was a Friday when the head nun had to take our class when our teacher was out sick. I was coughing and this irritated the class so I was sent to the infirmary. The room was rarely used although it was supposed to be a place for sick children. "Throughout the afternoon my cough got worse and I knew I had a fever because I was sweating profusely. No one came to check on me that evening. I was so scared. I cried and cried.

"I prayed that my mammy would come and take me home. I was left in the infirmary all night long. I kept having bad nightmares and fits of coughing.

"The next morning I could hear the other children pass by the infirmary on their way to breakfast. Still nobody came to check on me. I began to think I'd be better off dead. I felt suicidal. But then I thought who'd take care of the others. I was still sweating heavily and the smell of urine permeated the room as I'd wet the bed several times because I needed permission to go to the toilet. I cried so much.

"I cried again for my mammy to please come and take me home. I wanted somebody to know I was so ill, and to hug and comfort me."

But no one came to comfort Carmel that morning, or that afternoon, or when the long evening hours turned to night again. No one came to hug her or to wipe away her tears as she cried for her mother to hold her. She was seized by the fear that no one would ever find her and that she would die there, alone in the room. It was then, in her moment of greatest desolation, that the pitiless reality struck her with a fierce realization.

"Days came and went and still nobody called to see if I was alive or dead. This was strange as the infirmary was between a nun's cell and the bedroom of one of the lay staff. They must have heard me cough; I must have kept them awake. I wet the bed and slept on and off in my wet bedclothes for another night.

"The next morning it was Sunday. I knew because I could hear the children being lined up early for mass. Later I could hear children practising the violins. This class was held on a Sunday morning. Now I was very alarmed. If I missed Mass, what might happen to me? I never missed Mass before so I was sure I was going to die that afternoon and go to hell.

"I sneaked out to the toilet and the nun caught me on the way back. She knew by looking at me I was very unwell and brought me back to the infirmary. She had one of the girls change my bedclothes and my sheets. This was the one and only time I was not beaten for wetting my bed. A few hours later, the doctor came to see me. I heard him say that I had very bad croup and I would need medication and rest. It took a few weeks before I fully recovered.

"I knew after that that my mother wasn't coming back."

Desolate and alone now, Carmel steeled herself, like she had done when her brothers died. She must survive. She must think of her sisters. She must look out for them. Even take the pain for them.

"I recall one of the times I took a beating for my sister. I found her in a very distraught state on the corridor not too far from the head nun's office. She told me that she'd pulled another girl's hair. The lay staff sent her to the head nun. She saw me coming and told me what happened. I told her to go and hide in the toilets and instead I arrived at the nun's office. I told her that I'd been sent to see her because I had pulled a little girl's hair. She knew I was lying, as I'd forgotten to ask my sister the girl's name and number. She punished me severely. I was beaten several times on the back of the knuckles. I was in so much pain and crying so hard. I had to do double my quota of rosary bead making as well and recite the rosary silently for hours."

In a country blighted back then by poverty and emigration, reciting the rosary was central to people's lives and must have seemed like an alluring pact: the family that prayed together, stayed together. This promise, however, held no meaning for Carmel and did not keep her family together. But it is unlikely, as Irish families fingered their beads, that anyone wondered how these holy symbols had been fashioned. And if they had known, they would surely have recoiled in horror.

Carmel made many kinds of rosary beads at Goldenbridge but The Mother of Pearl rosaries, so often entwined around the fingers of the dead in Irish homes, were the most painful for Carmel to make. They were so fragile they would chip easily and the splinters would become embedded in her hands. Sometimes the pain became so excruciating she feared she would die.

"Making those pearl beads was the worst because they were so fragile. They were easily chipped and the splinters could get embedded in your hands. This was so painful. The wire was always cutting into our hands and fingers, resulting in blistering and boils. I was in so much pain I prayed to God to get me out before I died in that place."

But always she would think again of her sisters. She had to try to be strong for them, particularly when one of her sisters revealed a trauma to her. "My sister told me she had set the cupboard under the stairs on fire. I didn't know what was going on. She'd burned everything inside it, all the tools. Then she told me what had happened, why she'd lit the fire. She was crying. She told me she'd been assaulted in the cupboard (by a lay employee). He kept his tools in the cupboard. This was why she'd lit the fire and burned everything. We couldn't tell the nuns about the assault. They'd blame her and probably beat her, so we had to keep that to ourselves."

After the fire, the nuns put her sister on a sleeping tablet. Years later, Carmel discovered it was Mogadon. Her sister was then just 14 years old. "One day when I was approximately fifteen-and-a-half years old the head nun told me that my sister was going into hospital. I was ordered to accompany her with the nun. I didn't know it at the time, but we were going to the Central Mental Hospital in Dundrum. My sister was very quiet. The nun told me that my sister had a drug problem but I didn't believe she had and I hated the idea of yet another separation.

"My sister looked so vulnerable. I remember she had so much pain in her eyes. The walls of this hospital were so high. There was definitely no way out. In we went through those gigantic gates. We were brought into a sitting room surrounded by male inmates. My sister was the only female in the ward. I was very angry. But I had to contain myself out of fear I could be sent there too.

"When we returned to Goldenbridge the nun told me to pray for my sister's soul – and guess what – I did! The sense of betrayal that I felt that day still haunts me. Year later I discovered that my sister believed that I was the person who'd signed her into that hospital. That in itself created such a rift in our relationship but she understood when I explained to her in the late 90s that indeed I was never responsible for that incarceration and I was only a minor myself and did not have that control. I will carry this pain with me always. I know it will never heal."

Carmel's sister never fully recovered from the trauma of her years in Goldenbridge. She died suddenly in 2007 at the age of 50.

Amid all the traumas, and despite them, Carmel worked hard at school. But soon she discovered that being deemed bright in Goldenbridge had its disadvantages too. "I always came in the top three in the class. This was my downfall, as the lay teacher would not allow me to pass on to the next class. She wanted me to help her with the new children coming from first class to second class. It was only with publication of the Ryan Report that I discovered that this teacher had never qualified."

When Carmel finally moved into a nun's class, she was asked to spell the world ingredient. She didn't know it then but her whole future would be shaped by her answer. "It was only because I spelled the word correctly I was told that I was going out to Goldenbridge Secondary School."

Carmel was thrilled. She was now a step closer to freedom. "I was delighted. It would help me to get out too." But, in Goldenbridge Secondary School, success brought its own nightmares. No allowance was made for school and Carmel found herself struggling to fit in homework with making her quota of rosary beads and other chores.

"This proved to be my biggest nightmare, as I was struggling with my chores and making rosary beads as well. During my lunch break, I had to supervise the younger boys and later in the evening, I had to put them to bed. I couldn't go to bed myself unless every last one of them was asleep. I hated this job; the terrible isolation and the responsibility attached to it. After all, I was really only a child myself. I always missed breakfast; by the time I supervised the boys, breakfast time was over. I would then make sure they went to school and then run as fast as I could to secondary school. At lunchtime I'd run all the way back to school.

"After school I supervised the boys while trying to do my homework as well. Then I made rosary beads and once I finished I'd supervise the boys' until bedtime. At weekends, I scrubbed and cleaned in between minding the boys. I was always exhausted and I had great difficulty with my studies. It definitely felt like child slave labour. I felt I never had time to myself and as a result of this, I cannot relax today. I hope that one-day this huge anxiety will go away."

But Carmel triumphed against the odds, passing her Intermediate Cert and later going on to successfully complete her Leaving Cert, while living with her foster family, whom she met in August in 1972.

Carmel has a single keepsake from her years in Goldenbridge that she cherishes. But it didn't come from anyone in Goldenbridge or from any of her family or from any of her friends. It came from total strangers at Christmastime 44 years ago.

"It was late November 1970; a group of local young people in their early 20s came to visit us in Goldenbridge. They wanted to do something special for the teenagers. They asked us what we'd like for Christmas. This was something unheard of in Goldenbridge. There were no presents from Santa. When I was asked what I'd like, the other girls were shocked when I said I'd like a microscope. I always wanted to become a nurse or a doctor. My dad had medical books at home, which I used to try and read even though I didn't understand them. I got my microscope and I cherish this present to this very day."

In 1971, as she neared the end of her time in Goldenbridge, Carmel marked her 16th birthday. Looking back, she remembers it vividly because it was the only day there that she felt any degree of happiness. It would be short-lived, however.

"In 1971 things began to change. The nuns decided that the teenagers could have a party for their 16th birthday. I was taught cookery. I loved this class and it was the only time I felt really relaxed in Goldenbridge. The nun entered me into the Gas Company Cookery Competition. One year I won first place and I was invited to collect my certificate and attend a party with all the other competitors. I had a great time although I was very nervous in case anyone asked me what school I attended.

"On my 16th birthday with some of the others I enjoyed making a nice Victoria sponge cake. Then the nun told me to go and get changed, while the other girls arranged the room for the party. I was so thrilled as I skipped up the stairs. But then I met my sister. She was very upset. She told me that one of the girls had hit her. She asked me to sort it out. I found the girl and gave her a gentle puck. I couldn't believe it when I found out that she had told on me. As a result, I wasn't allowed to go to my own party. And I had to make extra rosary beads. I felt so unhappy and let down. I had been excited at the prospect of having a birthday party for the first time ever, and within minutes it was all over – no party."

Despite all that, Carmel still treasures the cards from that birthday over 40 years ago. "The birthday cards that I received from some of my friends in Goldenbridge on my 16th birthday I cherish to this day."

It was now 1972 and Carmel's life was about to change drastically. Soon she would leave Goldenbridge to face a world for which she was ill prepared.

"The turmoil of Goldenbridge had left me shattered."

The world outside was in as state of violent turmoil too. In January that year, 13 unarmed civilians had been shot dead in Derry when British troops opened fire on civil rights marchers in what became known as Bloody Sunday. A few days later, a protest in Dublin ended with the burning of the British Embassy. In July, nine people were killed in a series of IRA explosions in Belfast city centre. It was also the year that the people of Ireland voted to join the EEC.

For Carmel it was the year she got a summer job in a car accessories shop near Goldenbridge. It was there that she also found the chance of a new life one day when she met a young couple, the brother and sister-in-law of her employer. They also had a 3½-year-old son. "They knew that I was in Goldenbridge. A week before I was due back to Goldenbridge I babysat for them and they asked me if I'd like to stay with them on a permanent basis. I was very apprehensive and yet I thought it had to be a much better life than the place where I'd been incarcerated."

She was concerned, too, about the family she would be leaving behind. She had always tried to be there for them in Goldenbridge, giving them hope, taking their pain. She was plagued, too, by doubts about her own ability to function in this new world. Goldenbridge had terrorised her childhood, shattered her confidence, sundered her trust.

"I didn't trust the family, as this trust had been so severely damaged in Goldenbridge. I couldn't understand what this family saw in me. I was so scared they would send me back to Goldenbridge if I ever did anything wrong. Every day I brought them breakfast in bed because I thought this was something I had to do so they'd like me and want to keep me. This was something I felt inside me and was nothing to do with this wonderfully kind family. I had huge problems eating with the family, as I was not used to eating with adults. I was careful to eat small amounts of food because I felt this was necessary to save them money. But they were wonderful and they gave me everything I wanted. So it was nothing to do with them. It was all because my trust had been shattered."

But soon Carmel began to settle in and the family became her foster family. Looking back, she thinks they must have found her ways somewhat eccentric at the beginning. "My foster family must have thought I was mad, as I was always cleaning and tidying. I found it difficult to sit still for any length of time. After meals, I would swipe the crockery from underneath them and have them washed and dried as quick as they would bat an eyelid. I would reset the table as I did in Goldenbridge, and have it ready for the next meal. I was always scrubbing floors despite them reassuring me I didn't have to do these chores at all. They must have contemplated at some point had they fostered an eccentric child."

But the family were extremely supportive. Carmel began working two jobs to pay for her schoolbooks for the Leaving Cert and to help the family – though they discouraged this help. "They kept encouraging me to give up the jobs, but I was afraid to tell them why I felt the need to work. I'd convinced myself if I paid my way, they would definitely keep me. I have since learned that my family were very special people and this was a huge error on my part."

The fear of being sent back to Goldenbridge continued to haunt Carmel. Her visits to her sisters were constant reminders of that nightmare. "I was nervous that Goldenbridge could take me back anytime they wished. Yet I had to take the risk, as I was the only visitor to my sisters." It was a harrowing time.

Following Carmel's Leaving Cert, she dared to hope she could follow her dream of becoming a nurse. She asked the nuns for help. But where so much of her life had been shattered by the Sisters of Mercy, this dream too would die in Goldenbridge.

"I was aware that the Mercy nuns ran many of the hospitals, so I called to see the head nun at Goldenbridge to ask if she could help me to get into nursing. I was distraught when she told me she couldn't help me. She just wouldn't budge on it. I didn't have any confidence. I couldn't stand up for myself. My dreams and aspirations were broken in minutes. I became very anxious and then instead of nursing I ended up taking a menial office job. I still yearned to get into nursing but I didn't have the confidence to pursue this need inside of me. All that was shattered in Goldenbridge.

"My self-esteem was worse than ever. It took all I had to keep myself functioning just to get through a day. I had to push myself so hard to stay positive; otherwise, how would I visit my family? The struggle of building a life outside Goldenbridge, adapting to being free and in charge of my own destiny yet rooted with fear took its toll on me."

But she found enough confidence to look for another job. "This time I got one in a much nicer office, again as a clerical officer, and I liked the job." Carmel seemed a model worker. She worked very hard and got on well with everyone, but inside she was often consumed by fear.

One day and without any warning, Carmel's mother came back into her life. Her foster family called her and told here her mother was in the house and wanted to meet her. Fear gripped Carmel that this might somehow mean her foster family could send her back to Goldenbridge. She didn't want to see her mother but finally she agreed to meet her briefly because of the foster family's enormous kindness and support. "I remember her first words were 'Do I not get a hug?' No, I told her,

I don't know who you are anymore. Where were the hugs when my brothers, my sisters and I needed you?"

Carmel told her what had happened to her beloved brothers. Then, almost as suddenly as she had come, her mother left yet again. She said she was going back to England. She had married again there, she told Carmel, and had a daughter. Carmel was overwhelmed to discover she had a stepsister. She was shaken by the meeting and was relieved it was over.

Carmel remained with the same firm until she married in 1978 at the age of 23. Carmel and her husband have four children, who have grown into confident adults. Yet, almost from the start, Carmel suspected that her fears and insecurities had driven her into an unsuitable marriage. "Marriage was like a refuge, an escape. I couldn't be sent back to Goldenbridge. It was only through years of counselling, my voluntary work in the Aislinn Centre and my experience with survivors following the *Dear Daughter* programme in 1996 that I finally realised that, in order to protect my children and maintain my sanity, I would have to leave that marriage." Carmel and her husband divorced in 2000 but they have remained amicable in order to support their children.

This was time to lift other dark shadows from her life too, to try to find closure. Carmel decided it was time to find her mother and confront her.

In 2002, Carmel wrote to the Salvation Army in England, asking for their help in tracing her mother. Three years later, she received a reply from the Salvation Army in Manchester. The letter was devastatingly brief. "My mother told them she wanted no contact. It incensed me. I decided I'd go ahead myself and find her."

She remembered her mother telling her she was living in Manchester. With determination and doggedness, Carmel took on what seemed like an impossible task. Through a twist of fate, she finally found a lead through an archivist in Manchester that led her at last to her mother's address. She came up with a plan. "No-one else knew, just my ex-husband, my bosses and my children. Not even close friends because I was afraid I'd be talked out of it."

On July 9, 2005, exactly 40 years to the day since her mother had walked out on the family, Carmel left Dublin Airport on a flight to Manchester. There, in a one of those staggering co-incidences that life can throw up,

Carmel's brother called her as she got off the plane in Manchester. "He said he was in Manchester on business (from the Canaries). I blurted out that I was in Manchester too. Then I told him why. He asked to accompany me.

"We met and had breakfast and then got a taxi to where my mother lived. It was a very long road, a bit run down in parts. Finally, we arrived to the house and I knocked on the door. A man opened the door. We asked was our mother there. We explained who we were. He invited us in. We saw photos of Princess Diana everywhere and plenty of photos of our stepsister too and one of our mother. There were no other photographs. Not one of the eight children she had left behind in Ireland. No evidence of her life before."

The man told them their mother had gone shopping in a nearby town. Carmel asked for the photo of her mother, now in her 70s. Carmel made a decision.

"I was due to go to London to see my daughter on stage that evening. I decided to call and explain our dilemma. Then we changed all my flights for later in the evening. I had waited 40 years for this day and I wasn't going home yet. With the photo we'd been given we decided to visit the market town in a final attempt to try to find our mother. We walked around looking everywhere for about an hour. We decided we'd give it one last try and headed back again to my mother's house.

"This time my mother was at home. 'You know why we're here,' I told her. I asked her why she'd left us and why she hadn't returned. She remained silent with her head bowed down. Then she started talking about herself and her bad heart condition. She said she didn't know what had happened to us. I reminded her that I told her everything when she'd come to Dublin all of those years ago. And then I said 'You cannot say you didn't know.' She never said 'I'm sorry'. She'd married again. She'd had one child and she kept that child. We felt we didn't exist. As a parent, I couldn't understand this behaviour. And I never will. Eventually, I told her 'I'm getting up now and leaving. Don't worry, I'll never phone you or knock on your door again. I never want to see you. I have my own children whom I cherish'. We left. I felt relief. I knew finally I had closure."

Carmel's mother died a few years ago. Her children here were not informed. "When I heard she was dead I felt a sense of freedom."

The nightmares of Goldenbridge continue to haunt Carmel. There is little relief as she remembers the hunger, the cruelty, the deprivation and most of all the fear. "Sometimes I wake up gasping for air."

In those times of hopelessness and darkness, it is to the future that she tries to cling. Carmel has a grandson and a granddaughter now.

"They propel me forward. They are the light of my life."

10

STORY OF JOHN GRIFFIN

"It was a sea of barbarism"

The last time John Griffin saw his mother he was six weeks old. Now, 55 years later, after a long search, he had tracked her down to a house in Derby in England, hoping for answers that might rid him of the terrors of institutional child abuse that still haunted him.

He had been searching for his mother for more than 20 years and had finally found an address for her in England.

But that morning, as John Griffin travelled to Derby from Ireland, he was still not sure if he would find his mother.

She would now be almost 90. "Maybe she wasn't still at that address. Maybe she wasn't even still alive," he recalls thinking on that fateful day.

The address took him eventually to a rundown house on Bridge Street in Derby. It looked bleak even in the sunshine of a summer afternoon and John felt some trepidation as he approached the house. "I didn't know what might happen," he recalls.

"I knocked hard on the door. There was no response. But then, from upstairs, I heard a window opening. A woman put her head out.

"'No lodgers,' she shouted, 'go away.'"

John began to think he was at the wrong house. "I was about to turn and leave but instead I looked up at the woman at the window."

They could clearly see each other's faces now in the bright light of the early afternoon.

"'Come back here,' she shouted. 'You're John, aren't you?'

'I've been waiting for you. Come in.'"

When she opened the door, she was smiling at him, telling him that the week before, a fortune teller had told her he'd finally come.

"'I knew you'd come. I was waiting to die till I saw you,'" Annie Griffin told her son.

But there were no hugs. Too much pain had been endured.

"'I've been waiting for you for a long time,'" his mother told him as they sat at her kitchen table.

Her son, too, had been waiting a long time. And now he wanted answers. But what he learned next stunned him.

She told him he had four older siblings, three sisters and one brother. His brother's name was Peter and his sisters were Mary, Josey and Annie – though Annie was already dead.

John found it difficult to elicit much information from his now ailing mother. She was vague about their lives and her own.

There would be fragments of answers – she told him that he had been taken from her at six weeks old; that this had happened at St Patrick's Mother and Baby Home in Dublin, where she'd worked downstairs while he was upstairs, though she never saw him; and finally that she'd left St Patrick's for England, alone.

By this time, it appears his father, James Griffin, a cattle drover, who spent any money the family had on drink, was already dead. Later his mother married again and at some point brought her other children to England. But not John, for reasons he would never discover. "She might have planned it, I think, but a lot happened in her life and she didn't or maybe wasn't able to."

John was thus left behind in Ireland where he was to spend a terrifying childhood, first in a Dublin convent and then in Baltimore Fishing School in West Cork, and he would never see his mother again until 55 years later on that afternoon in Derby in the summer of 1989.

The reunion seems to have been infused, for both of them, with a sense of triumph, of achievement against the odds, rather than emotional attachment.

"I knew we'd meet and she knew we'd meet. The satisfaction was more for her, but it was a vindication for both of us."

While his mother was not able to answer many of his questions, she did give John a treasured possession: a colour photograph she'd kept of both of them together. It means the world to him. "Evidence she cared, I suppose."

It was taken, she'd written on the back, when John was six weeks old.

He smiles when he holds it now. And, indeed, it seems an idyllic family photo of mother and son in a sunny back garden at the height of summer.

His mother is sitting on a chair, with John on her lap, and all around them red roses are in bloom.

But soon mother and baby would be separated and this would be the last such picture of them together.

"She'd been waiting to give it to me," John says, smiling at the photograph and at the remarkable resemblance between Annie Griffin then and John Griffin now.

He is happy to have it, happy that she'd kept it, happy, above all, that she'd lived long enough to share the memory with him.

Mother and son would spend three weeks together in Derby. "Three very happy weeks." Then, one month later, John Griffin learned that his ailing mother had died.

Annie Griffin had managed to live long enough for her to see her son and for him to find her. John, who is now almost 80, still marvels at that, that she'd put off dying until they met.

"She'd postponed her dying. Despite all that had happened, those weeks were the happiest time," he recalls.

Subsequently, in England, John also met his two surviving sisters and his brother and their families but does not see them now and is not close to any of them: "We'd never seen each other before. They're living their lives. I have mine."

Today, John Griffin lives his life in Skibbereen, just 20 minutes' drive from Baltimore. He clearly enjoys living in the splendour of West Cork.

But is it not unsettling to live so close to the scene of the horrors of his childhood?

Here again, it seems, his love for West Cork is mixed with that sense of survival against the odds, that sense of triumph over adversity.

"In Baltimore, they never let us go to Skibbereen. I always wanted to see it. And when I did I liked it, so I stayed."

He has travelled much of the world over the years, but always feels at home in Skibbereen. Yet his original home was not in Cork but in the heart of Dublin.

John Griffin was born in July 1934 in the Coombe Hospital, Dublin, and at six weeks old was transferred to St Patrick's Mother and Baby home in the city, where he and his mother were briefly together. Almost five years later, in February 1939, he was transferred south of the city to St Philomena's convent.

Some children had visitors there, but not John. "When I was about four, I asked in the convent if I had a mother and father and the nun said they were dead."

It was a common lie that was told to many children in institutions across Ireland. John Griffin, a dignified, quiet, articulate man, who appears without bitterness or anger when he speaks, uses a chilling analogy to describe such lies. "It was like a form of ethnic cleansing," he says.

"If you were abandoned or if a woman had an illegitimate child she died in their eyes, her children too. That's why they treated us like they did. We were to pay for the sins of our parents. And pay we did."

But it must be so much harder to make sense of such cruelty, when you're not yet five and a nun begins to make your life a daily hell.

"For those who wet their beds, she gave orders to the cleaners who came in each day that we were to be ducked in ice cold baths of water.

"If you wet your bed you were held tightly by your small hands and feet. We were pushed naked under the ice-cold water four or five times. Often we were held under the water until we were almost out of breath. We were pulled out gasping for breath and blue from the cold. We were petrified.

"Then that night you reported in your nightshirt for a beating with her cane on your bare behind. You usually got three or four strokes."

John Griffin will never forget the cruelty of that nun and over 70 years later, he still hears in his head "the swishing sound of her cane." He remembers, too, the scissors she carried.

"She carried a very large scissors and this was used on us when she didn't have her cane on her."

John was to encounter some kindness. "There was one Sister, she was a gentle person, and often when she was changing our clothes she'd notice we were always black and blue. 'Did Sister X do that to you?' she'd ask. I'd look up at her and say nothing, and start to cry. I never gave her an answer. There was no need. She showed us love and understanding."

But what still haunts him is the unrelenting cruelty. "By the time we left the convent for Baltimore the devil had been beaten out of us, as they saw it, and replaced by a fear of God.

"But little did we know that worse was yet to come."

In May 1945, two months before he turned 11, John Griffin, along with about 12 other boys from St Philomena's, was transferred over 300km from Dublin to Baltimore Fishing School, in West Cork.

Worse was indeed to come.

After a long train journey from Dublin, they changed at Cork and then went on the old train line that took them directly to Baltimore and the Fishing School. But even before he left the train at Baltimore, the young boy would see the terrors that awaited him.

"It was very late when the train arrived but it was still bright enough to make out a lot of boys my own age, in rags, no shoes, or socks, and an old man holding a stick.

"I had still not left the train and noticed he started raining blows on the boys. They could not defend themselves from the blows. I started to cry." He was beating the boys out of the way of the new boys getting off the train.

John soon found out that this man was the night watchman and at night, he would beat any boys he caught out of bed.

There were other terrors too. The dormitory was rat infested. "The rats were running up and down the dormitory all night which frightened me even more.

"The dormitory was a place where boys cried all night long. They were very hungry and cold and had to lie on their wet beds. And you were never sure when you'd get a blow from the night watchman's stick as he prowled the dormitories looking for a victim."

When the boys arrived, their heads were shaved except for a small quiff. "This was used to drag or hold you for a beating."

Baltimore Fishing School opened in 1886 and was unique among the industrial schools in Ireland in that it was not run by a religious order but was under diocesan control.

It was staffed by two to three priests from the Diocese of Ross, and a few lay workers. During the five years that John spent at the school, there were about 140 boys. The Laffoy Commission, which investigated the school and published its report in 2004, described conditions there as "unbelievable".

The commission heard testimony from over a dozen people from the school. Among them was John Griffin, though none were named at the time.

The life they described "was so harsh and deprived by the standards of today, as to verge on the unbelievable," Justice Mary Laffoy's report said and concluded that their accounts were credible.

John says they had hardly any clothes and those they did have were bug ridden. He recalls boys helping each other to pick out the bugs "like monkeys do".

But it was the constant hunger that was the worst.

"We were hungry and went to bed hungry, all through my years I spent there. We were like a pack of wild animals. If you found a bone, you didn't bury it like a dog; you took it back to your bed and kept it.

"The hunger, cold and filth were the hardest to endure. I thought about the cleanliness and food at St Philomena's, and the morning drownings didn't seem as bad as the squalor and hunger in Baltimore."

Breakfast for the young boys consisted of a slice of dry bread and cocoa. Dinner was usually watery soup, a potato and a little meat, but the meat was often rotten and infested with maggots, John says. The boys in charge of the meat would often take it down to the sea first to wash it. Supper, like breakfast, was a slice of dry bread and cocoa.

"The last meal of the day was at 5.30, bread and cocoa. You dare not ask for more as this was met with a blow from the priest's stick. He would be walking up and down the length of the refectory.

"We were so hungry that we would escape and beg for any kind of scraps of bread from the fishing boats down at the pier."

His memory of his Confirmation day there is also one of hunger and of being beaten. "We were beaten on our Confirmation day for going out begging."

Sometimes they would sneak out to the town to steal bread. "The vans from Skibbereen town were loaded with bread and we'd steal what we could carry and take it to pieces like snarling dogs to satisfy our hunger."

Their hunger would overcome their fear of the punishment that awaited them if they were caught.

"The priest blew a whistle every five to 10 minutes and you had to be very quick to get back. If you were caught, an example was made of you in front of the school.

"A special stage was erected and punishment was witnessed by every boy. You were put across the stage, pants pulled well down and held tightly by your small hands in a vice grip and given 10 strokes of the cane. Your only crime was hunger and a will to survive."

As he recalls the hunger, John points out the fields around Baltimore where the boys would steal and hide vegetables in pits. "We stole mangles, turnips, potatoes from farmers' fields. We would take some of our goods to bed, as 5.30 was the last crust of bread you got. It was always very sad to hear boys crying who didn't have any." All the vegetables were eaten raw. "The mangles were particularly sweet," he says.

There was little respite, even on Christmas day. "We never got any sort of toys or games for Christmas, just the usual bread and cocoa and even on that day we searched for food in the village."

Washing dirty sheets was another nightmare that John recalls vividly.

"We were petrified when told to report to the woman who was in charge, to wash sheets. We were expected to wash the sheets in ice-cold water; it was just impossible to get them really clean. You held each sheet up for her inspection, high above your head, and prayed you wouldn't get a savage blow from her.

"She was an evil, wicked woman and I will never forget her, even to this day."

Such suffering left deep emotional scars. "Down through the years, I found it was women who had made my young life hell, as I didn't expect it from them, at the convent and at Baltimore. And any thoughts I ever had of getting married were ruined by these cruel people when we were small and helpless. Men were to be my tormentors later."

Learning in Baltimore was also imbued with fear and, along with the physical and emotional scars, the boys would face life almost totally uneducated.

"I was petrified to go to school as the masters were very cruel," John says, recalling a particular form of brutality used by one lay teacher, Master Foley, now deceased, against the boys.

"Master Foley's favourite, perverted punishment for any boy who could not read or write was called the aeroplane.

"The frightened boy's jersey was wrapped tightly around his head to hold him steady and to muffle any cries he would make and his short pants was pulled down around his legs to hold him steady.

"The master stood at 5ft 7in and the boy was raised to his height. The strap was a barber's leather strap. He had sewn pieces of lead into the end of it and with all the strength he could muster, he would lay the strap hard on the boy's backside until we were black and blue.

"This savage punishment was carried out all through my six years in his class."

John Griffin is haunted by the memory of what happened to one boy who suffered this punishment.

"I well remember a very frail boy receiving this savage beating and who passed out. He was taken away and we never saw him again and we learned later that had died of his injuries."

John says that some boys also suffered sexual abuse from lay workers but not from any of the three priests.

When the then Bishop of Ross failed to make any real improvements to the school, the Department of Education finally closed it down in 1950. By then John was due to leave anyway because he was 16 and the State's capitation grant to the school ended for the boys at that age.

"We were informed we would be leaving Baltimore school, as we had just turned 16. After nearly six long suffering years we would now face a world about which we knew nothing and for which we were totally unprepared."

Many went to work for local farmers in West Cork.

John recalls the farmers coming to the school and choosing the boys to work for them "as if they were inspecting cattle at a fair".

Life as a farm labourer was both tough and cruel. "One minute I would be treated like the pet dog and next I would get a yard brush across the back for being lazy."

Some boys were treated so badly by the farmers that they ran away and went back to Baltimore. But they were beaten so savagely when they came back that they never did so again. John Griffin saw one boy being beaten mercilessly by the priest in charge. "He was kicked all the way out of the school yard and down the road," he says, pointing to the spot where he was when he saw this happening.

Most of the boys never got paid by the farmers. "It was long hours of hardship and no pay." John started work at 6 am and often worked till 11 pm. He got paid once – in a matchbox. It was a sixpenny piece for one month's work and the farmer said that it was in a matchbox so that John wouldn't lose it.

Another time he got 2/6, "but that must have been a mistake," John smiles, "because I didn't get paid after that for a few months." He is able to smile at it now, but back then, John says most of the boys felt like "Irish slaves."

John Griffin decided after about a year of this that there must be more to life. "At least I wanted to try to find out, so I escaped."

He got as far as Cork city but couldn't find work and soon ended up begging on the streets of the city. After a few weeks, he saw an ad for a helper at a school for the blind. He went to the school and managed to get the job. "I was able to live there and I got food and some money. It was a case of the blind leading the blind," he smiles, "but I was happy there."

Then he heard that the Irish Army was recruiting and he decided to join up in about 1952. After a few years in the Irish Army, he read about a recruitment programme for the New Zealand Army. He wanted to see other parts of the world. He decided it was time to leave Ireland.

He kept himself on the move. From New Zealand he went to Australia, to parts of Asia, to England, where he spent a period with the British Merchant Navy, and then back again to Ireland and finally to Skibbereen in West Cork.

He was busy, he was enjoying life, and for a time he succeeded in numbing the terrors of his childhood. But not for long.

"I was able to block some of these things out, but as you get older they start to come back to you more clearly."

He was in his late 20s now. He wanted more answers. He decided it was time to try to look for his mother. But it would be a long search.

He would spend more than 20 years, on and off, looking for clues. Eventually, he found an address for her at Cork Street in Dublin. But by this time, the house she'd lived in was gone. He decided to knock on a few doors and ask about Annie Griffin.

He would make an extraordinary discovery. At one house, he found a neighbour who knew Annie Griffin. "She was an elderly lady. She brought me into her house. She said she had something to show me.

"She opened a drawer and in it she had letters from my mother. She'd been writing to her in England and had an address for her in Derby."

He made plans as soon as he could do so to travel to England and there, in the city of Derby in the summer of 1989, in a rundown house on Bridge Street, John Griffin would finally find his mother just two months before she died.

The terrors that have haunted John Griffin's life have eased over the years. He has found friends. He has helped others in their suffering. A few years ago, he was awarded a medal that he treasures, for his work with Gorta to combat world hunger.

He has organised meetings of the "Baltimore boys", linking up with some in Australia and England, and has helped to erect a memorial near the site of the Baltimore Fishing School, remembering all those who were in the school from 1930 to 1950.

In one of those dark twists of irony, the site of the old Fishing School is now a thriving leisure centre. But the original school courtyard still remains as part of it.

As we drive into the centre, John Griffin speaks of the horror he feels that that such cruelty was tolerated in Baltimore and similar institutions across Ireland run by the religious.

"If their kind were to operate in today's Ireland they would be lynched. And yet their actions went unchecked in that sea of barbarism."

He believes that many priests, brothers and nuns in those days had no vocations. "They were responding to family pressure to take up religious vows. They entered without religious vocations and later they were to resent being denied motherhood and being imprisoned within the institutions until death," he suggests.

Not alone was it tolerated, he says, but the cruelty and abuse was usually ignored by Church and State. John Griffin likens both to "an army of Pontius Pilates washing their hands."

"Sometimes I wonder what connection, if any, there is between Catholicism and Christianity. When I left the school, I was convinced there was none. One does not easily forget such things. I saw terror in the eyes of the boys each day at school."

And he still does, even now, on the year of his 80th birthday.

"It has stayed with me down through the years," he says.

"I still cry for them, often."